Great Patchwork:
Stars and Stripes

Great Patchwork:
Stars and Stripes

BETTER HOMES AND GARDENS® BOOKS

DES MOINES, IOWA

Better Homes and Gardens® Books, an imprint of Meredith® Books:
President, Book Group: Joseph J. Ward
Vice President, Editorial Director: Elizabeth P. Rice

Executive Editor: Maryanne Bannon
Senior Editor: Carol Spier
Assistant Editor: Bonita Eckhaus
Selections Editor: Eleanor Levie
Technical Editor: Cyndi Marsico
Technical Assistant: Diane Rode Schneck
Copy Editor: Mary Butler
Book Design: Beth Tondreau Design/ M. Leo Albert, Daniel Rutter,
    Beth Tondreau, Mary A. Wirth
Technical Artist: Phoebe Adams Gaughan
Photographer: Steven Mays
Photo Stylist: Susan Piatt
Production Manager: Bill Rose

The editors would like to thank the Village of Waterloo museum,
Stanhope, New Jersey, and The Inn at Millrace Pond, Hope, New Jersey,
for sharing their premises for photography. Thanks also to Susan Parrish Antiques,
New York City, and Michael Goyda American Country Furniture, E. Petersburg,
Pennsylvania, for their kind assistance in the search for quilts to include in this volume.

Contents

Red, white and blue are forever dear to the hearts of American quilters, who have used them to make commemorative and centennial quilts since the country was young. In this book you'll find eight quilts that set stars and stripes waving over wall or bed. Turn to the CHANGING COLORS *and* CHANGING SETS *features and you'll see that these quilts are based on wonderful patchwork patterns that you can make in any color you wish. Most are quite easy to re-create; some, like the Country Patches Flag, were commissioned especially for this book, while others, like the Fireworks, are unusual old quilts. For a wonderful salute to America and a new take on quiltmaking tradition, turn to the* EXPERT'S CHALLENGE, *a contemporary sampler of patriotic blocks. Hurrah!*

These symbols, found on the opening page of each project, identify suggested levels of experience needed to make the projects in this book. However, you will see within these pages many interpretations of each project, and the editors hope you will find for each something easily achievable or challenging, as you wish.

New Quilter   *Confident Quilter*   *Expert Quilter*

Striped Sashing Quilt

This quilt is about one hundred years old and the pattern was most likely created by its maker. The simple trellis design of stripes and diamonds has an almost whirligig energy. The allover quilting pattern is just a diamond grid, but the plain blocks could be striking filled with a more elaborate quilting pattern. If you would like a more challenging project, think of setting this sashing around pieced blocks. The striped portion of the sashing can be strip-pieced or cut from striped fabric.

Note: All dimensions except for binding are finished size.
Amounts for full/queen are given in parentheses.

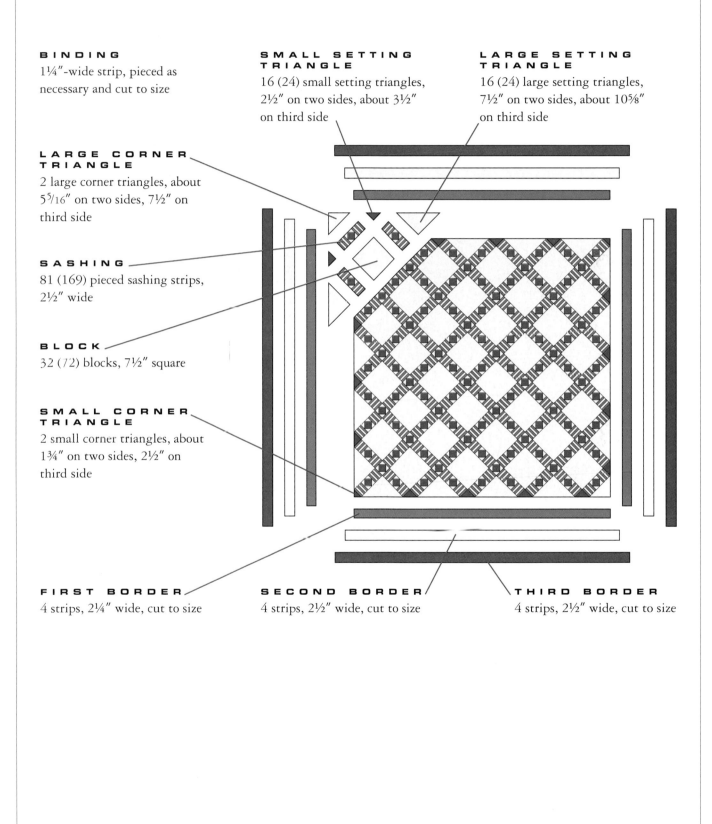

BINDING
1¼"-wide strip, pieced as necessary and cut to size

SMALL SETTING TRIANGLE
16 (24) small setting triangles, 2½" on two sides, about 3½" on third side

LARGE SETTING TRIANGLE
16 (24) large setting triangles, 7½" on two sides, about 10⅝" on third side

LARGE CORNER TRIANGLE
2 large corner triangles, about 5⁵⁄₁₆" on two sides, 7½" on third side

SASHING
81 (169) pieced sashing strips, 2½" wide

BLOCK
32 (72) blocks, 7½" square

SMALL CORNER TRIANGLE
2 small corner triangles, about 1¾" on two sides, 2½" on third side

FIRST BORDER
4 strips, 2¼" wide, cut to size

SECOND BORDER
4 strips, 2½" wide, cut to size

THIRD BORDER
4 strips, 2½" wide, cut to size

Note: Sizes and amounts for full/queen are given in parentheses.

Yardages are based on 44″ fabric. Prepare templates, if desired, referring to drafting schematics. Cut strips and patches following schematics and chart; see *Using the Cutting Charts*, page 88. Cut binding as directed below. Except for drafting schematics, which give finished sizes, all dimensions include ¼″ seam allowance and strips include extra length, unless otherwise stated. (NOTE: Angles on all patches are either 45° or 90°.)

DIMENSIONS

FINISHED BLOCK
7½″ square; about 10⅝″ diagonal

FINISHED QUILT
About 78″ (106¼″) square

MATERIALS

☐ MUSLIN SOLID
5½ (7¼) yds.

■ RED SOLID
2½ (3¼) yds.

■ NAVY PRINT
2½ (3¼) yds.

BINDING
½ yd. lt. blue solid, cut and pieced to make a 1¼″ × 340″ (1¼″ × 460″) strip.

BACKING *
5¼ (10) yds.

BATTING *

THREAD

*Backing and batting should be cut and pieced as necessary so they are at least 4″ larger than quilt top on all sides, then trimmed to size after quilting.

DRAFTING SCHEMATICS

(No seam allowance added)

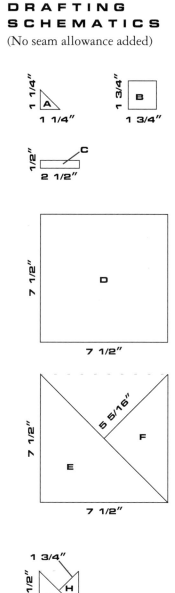

GREAT TIME-SAVING TIP

You can use a single fabric with 1/2″-wide stripes (1 3/4 yds. for twin, 2 1/4 yds. for full/queen) instead of strip-piecing two different fabrics for each striped sashing unit. Cut each unit 3″ square.

FIRST CUT			SECOND CUT	
Fabric and Yardage	Number of Pieces	Size	Number of Pieces	Shape
PLAIN PATCHES				
Muslin Solid 3 (4) yds.	6	2⅛″ × 81″ (2⅛″ × 108″)	452 (596)	A[1]
	7 (15)	8″ × 40″	32 (72)	D
	4 (5)	5¹⁵⁄₁₆″ × 40″	16 (24)	E
	1	4⅜″ × 20″	2	F
Red Solid[2]	3	2¼″ × 90″ (2¼″ × 117″)	113 (149)	B
	1	2⅛″ × 50″ (2⅛″ × 70″)	16 (24)	G
	1	1⅞″ × 10″	2	H
FIRST BORDER[3]				
Navy Print 2½ (3¼) yds.	2	2¾″ × 72″ (2¾″ × 100″)		
	2	2¾″ × 76″ (2¾″ × 104″)		
SECOND BORDER[3]				
Muslin Solid 2½ (3¼) yds.	2	3″ × 76″ (3″ × 104″)		
	2	3″ × 81″ (3″ × 109″)		
THIRD BORDER[3]				
Red Solid 2½ (3¼) yds.	2	3″ × 81″ (3″ × 109″)		
	2	3″ × 86″ (3″ × 114″)		

[1] Cut A's from remainder of fabric from second border.
[2] Cut B's, G's and H's from remainder of fabric from third border.
[3] Reserve remainder of fabric for cutting patches.

FIRST CUT			SECOND CUT		
Fabric and Yardage	Number of Pieces	Size	Method	Number of Pieces	Shape
STRIP-PIECED PATCHES[1]					
Navy Print and Muslin Solid	18 (30)	1″ × 81″ (1″ × 108″)		162 (338)	C/C/C/C/C
	12 (20)	1″ × 81″ (1″ × 108″)			

[1] Cut strips from remainder of fabric from first and second borders; see also the *Great Time-Saving Tip*, page 8. Join strips lengthwise, alternating colors as shown.

CUTTING SCHEMATICS

(Seam allowance included)

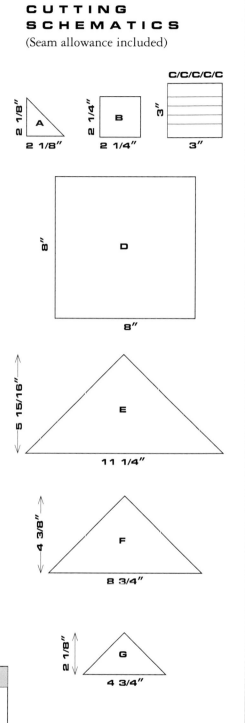

The size of this quilt can be adjusted easily from twin to full/queen if the number of components is increased to make four additional rows of blocks and four additional rows of sashing.

TWIN
32 blocks, quilt center about 63½″ square

FULL/QUEEN
72 blocks, quilt center about 91¾″ square

Sashing

Directions are given below for twin. Differing amounts for full/queen are given in parentheses.

1. Join 4 A's to a B to make a square-in-a-square. Make 113 (149).

2. Join 2 C/C/C/C/C squares to a square-in-a-square to make a sashing strip. Make 81 (169).

Quilt Center

Arrange units as shown. Join units to make rows.
Join rows.

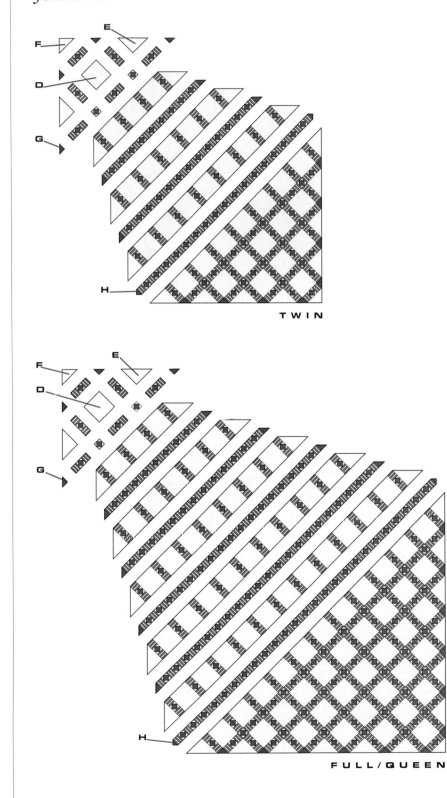

TWIN

FULL/QUEEN

Borders

Join borders to quilt center, first shorter strips at top and bottom, then longer strips at sides. Complete first border before proceeding to second, then third.

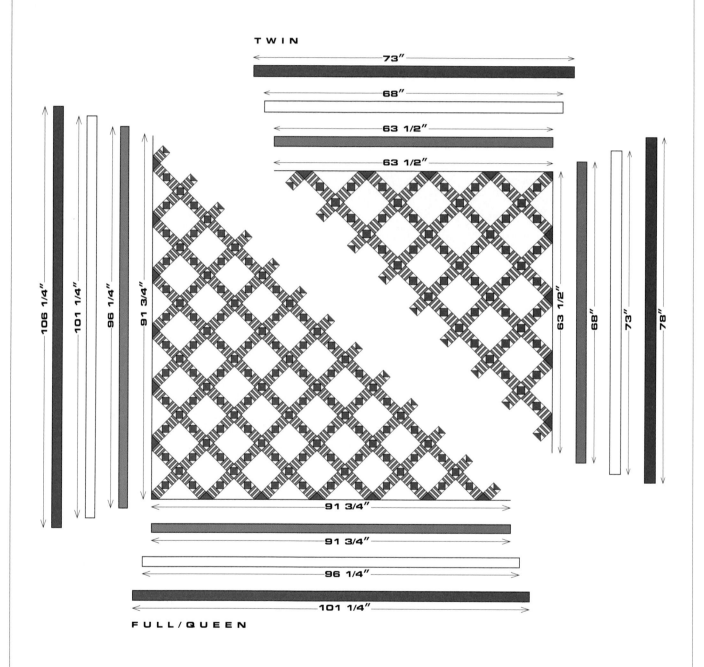

TWIN

FULL/QUEEN

Finishing

The quilting design used in this antique is a simple diagonal grid. The diamonds on one diagonal half of the quilt are perpendicular to those on the other half.

1. Divide quilt diagonally along the line indicated by the arrow in the second illustration. Mark quilting design on quilt top. Do not mark seams.

- *For quilt center:* Mark vertical lines 1″ apart on D's and E's on first half of quilt, using corners of C's as a guide. Mark horizontal lines on second half of quilt in same manner.
- *For quilt center and borders:* Mark 45° diagonal lines in opposite directions on each half of quilt. Draw lines 1″ apart and parallel to block edges.

2. Prepare batting and backing.

3. Assemble quilt layers.

4. Quilt on all marked lines and in-the-ditch on sashing seams to make diagonal lines continuous on each half of quilt.

5. Trim batting and backing to 1¼″ beyond outermost seam line.

6. Bind quilt edges.

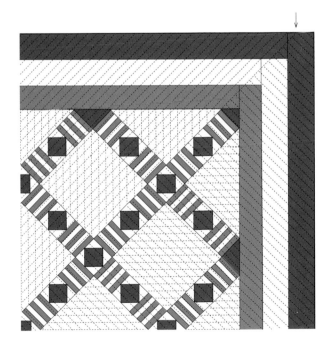

The way you place color in this pattern will change its appearance as much as the palette you use. Note how different it looks when you make the plain blocks the same color as the small squares. If you make the perpendicular bands of sashing from contrasting colors, you will create a plaid.

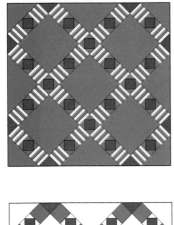
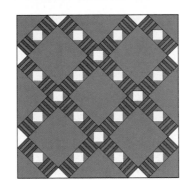
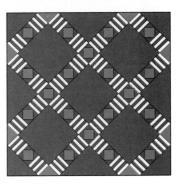

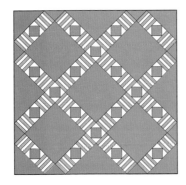
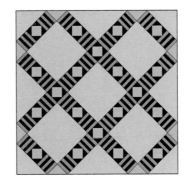
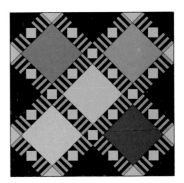

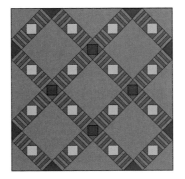
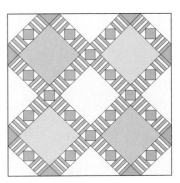

Photocopy this page, then create your own color scheme using colored pencils or markers. Refer to the examples shown, or design a unique arrangement to match your decor or please your fancy. Experiment to see what happens when you make alternate or adjacent plain blocks from different colors.

Because the sashing is the element of interest in this design, you really cannot create another pattern by changing the set of the components. You can, however, work with fewer components and use this pattern to make a smaller project.

♦ *For a pillow:* Combine 1 block, 4 sashing strips, 4 small setting triangles and 4 large corner triangles, and add a single 1"-wide border to make a pillow about 16" square. For fun, replace the plain block with the star block from the Little Flag Wallhanging on page 28, enlarging it first by adding a single 3/4"-wide border around it.

♦ *For a wallhanging:* Combine 5 blocks, 8 pieced sashing strips, 4 large setting triangles, 8 small setting triangles, and 4 large corner triangles to make a wallhanging about 28 1/4" square. If you add borders as for the large quilt, your wallhanging will be about 42 3/4" square.

If you arrange the components in a straight set you can easily make a quilt of almost any size. Just remember that the length of each edge will be a multiple of 10" (one block + one sashing width) plus 2 1/2" (one sashing width to complete the pattern) plus any borders you might wish to add. Here are some examples without borders:

  9 blocks in a 3 × 3 layout = 32 1/2"-square wallhanging
24 blocks in a 4 × 6 layout = 42 1/2" × 62 1/2" crib quilt
63 blocks in a 7 × 9 layout = 72 1/2" × 92 1/2" twin quilt
90 blocks in a 9 × 10 layout = 92 1/2" × 102 1/2" full/queen quilt

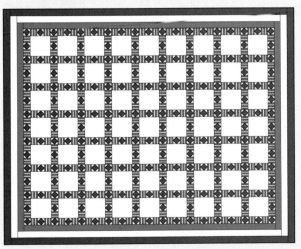

If you add 3 borders (as shown in the diagonal set quilt) to the 7 × 9 layout, you will have an 87 1/2" × 107" full/queen quilt.

Country Patches Flag Quilt

BY SUELLEN COCHRANE WASSEM

The effect of this clever Nine-Patch and Triangle Square interpretation of the Stars and Stripes is that of a flag waving in the breeze on a hazy day. Suellen Wassem has designed a charming—and very easy—project in muted patriotic tones, but you can just as happily interpret it in clearer hues. Turn to page 25 to see how, by choosing other color values, or by arranging colors differently, you can transform this pattern in unexpected ways, creating a plaid or even a field of stylized Christmas trees.

Note: All dimensions except for binding are finished size.

NAVY TRIANGLE SQUARE BLOCK
4 blocks, 6″ square

BINDING
1″-wide strip, pieced as necessary and cut to size

NAVY 9-PATCH BLOCK
5 blocks, 6″ square

ECRU 9-PATCH BLOCK
11 blocks, 6″ square

ECRU TRIANGLE SQUARE BLOCK
13 blocks, 6″ square

RED 9-PATCH BLOCK
16 blocks, 6″ square

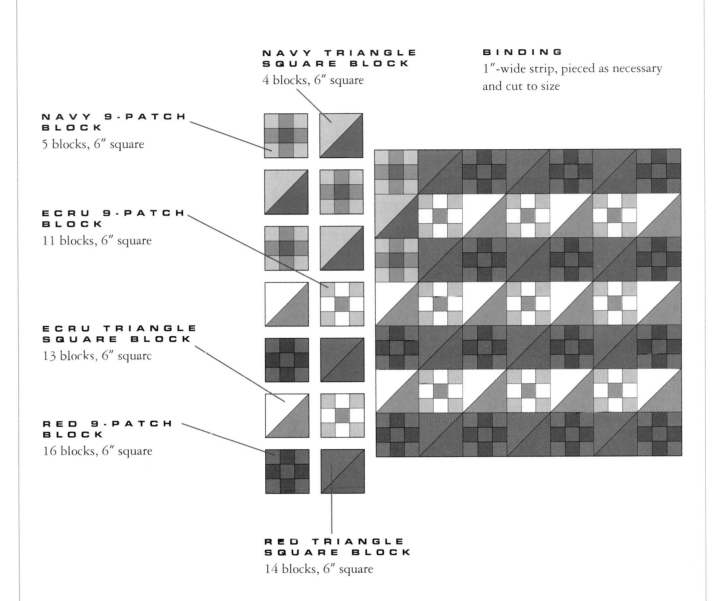

RED TRIANGLE SQUARE BLOCK
14 blocks, 6″ square

GREAT ACCESSORY IDEA

You can make a Country Patches pillow or small wallhanging by reducing the finished size of the components. If you reduce the block pieces 50% (A = 1″ square; B/B = 3″ square), you will have a 27″ × 21″ quilt front.

For a pillow, assemble the layers, quilt them, add a pillow back, then stuff with fiberfill.

For a small wallhanging, assemble the quilt in the same manner as for the full-size wallhanging, or omit the binding and display the wallhanging in a frame.

9-Patch Blocks

1. Join 3 ecru A/A/A strips as shown to make 11 blocks.

**FINISHED
ECRU BLOCK**

2. Join 3 red A/A/A strips as shown to make 16 blocks.

**FINISHED
RED BLOCK**

3. Join 3 navy A/A/A strips as shown to make 5 blocks.

**FINISHED
NAVY BLOCK**

Quilt Center

1. Arrange navy blocks as shown, alternating 9-patches and triangle squares.

2. Join 3 red triangle squares and 3 red 9-patches to make 2 short strips.

3. Join 3 ecru 9-patches and 3 ecru triangle squares to make one short strip.

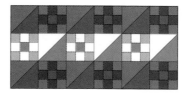

4. Join short strips, alternating colors and block types, to make a short striped field.

5. Join 5 ecru triangle squares and 4 ecru 9-patches, alternating blocks, to make 2 long strips.

6. Join 5 red 9-patches and 4 red triangle squares to make 2 long strips.

7. Join long strips, alternating colors and block types, to make a long striped field.

8. Arrange units as shown. Join units to make 2 rows. Join rows.

Finishing

1. Prepare batting and backing.

2. Assemble quilt layers.

3. Quilt in-the-ditch on all diagonal seams.

4. Trim batting and backing to 1/4″ beyond outermost seam line.

5. Bind quilt edges.

GREAT SIZING TIP

Because this pattern will repeat continuously no matter how many blocks are placed in each row or column, you can plan your quilt to be almost any size you wish. Just remember that the length of each edge will be a multiple of 6″ (one block). Note that not all configurations will work as flags. Note also, because this is a two-block pattern, that if each row and column of your layout contains an even number of blocks, the corner blocks will not be the same.

   9 blocks in a 3 × 3 layout = 18″-square wallhanging

   63 blocks in a 7 × 9 layout = 42″ × 54″ crib quilt (shown)

   176 blocks in an 11 × 16 layout = 66″ × 96″ twin quilt

   224 blocks in a 14 × 16 layout = 84″ × 96″ full/queen quilt

While Suellen Wassem's clever arrangement of muted reds, whites and blues gives her quilt the look of a flag waved by the wind, you can make this simple pattern in any palette you like. It will look remarkably different if you use fewer colors, or fewer values of each color. It would also be charming as a scrap quilt.

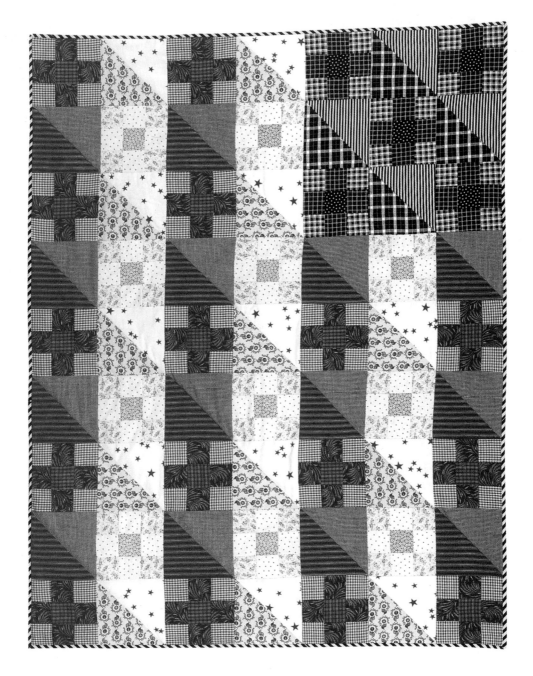

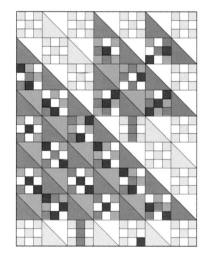
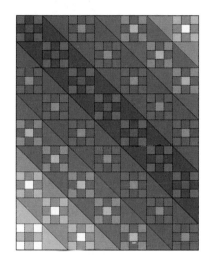

Photocopy this page, then create your own color scheme using colored pencils or markers. Refer to the examples shown, or design a unique arrangement to match your decor or please your fancy. Experiment to see what happens when you change the relative positions of the different colors or color values.

This quilt is made from two classic blocks, and you can, of course, use either one alone, set with sashing or plain setting squares, to make any number of familiar patterns. But you can also arrange the two blocks in other ways, and some of these can be made even more interesting with the addition of sashing.

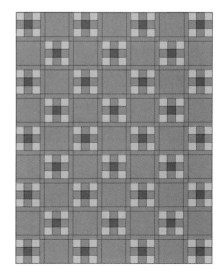

Little Flag Wallhanging

BY SANDRA SIKORSKI

A graphic designer and new convert to quilting, Sandra used scraps left over from a baby quilt to raise this flag. She chose a single Ohio Star block to give her small piece dramatic punch, and unified it with coordinated fabrics in tiny, allover prints. The wide border adds balance and keeps the design from seeming trite. As shown, this little flag is the perfect size for a pillow or placemat, but you might also think of doubling the size of each component to make a larger hanging.

Note: All dimensions except for binding are finished size.

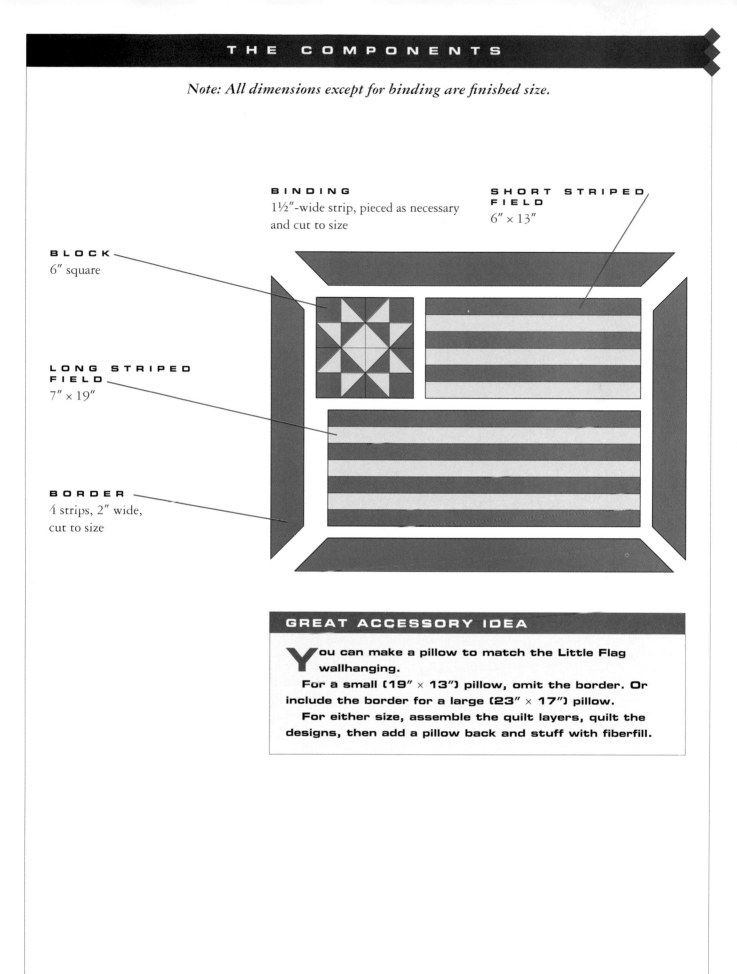

BINDING
1½"-wide strip, pieced as necessary and cut to size

SHORT STRIPED FIELD
6" × 13"

BLOCK
6" square

LONG STRIPED FIELD
7" × 19"

BORDER
4 strips, 2" wide, cut to size

GREAT ACCESSORY IDEA

You can make a pillow to match the Little Flag wallhanging.

For a small (19" × 13") pillow, omit the border. Or include the border for a large (23" × 17") pillow.

For either size, assemble the quilt layers, quilt the designs, then add a pillow back and stuff with fiberfill.

Yardages are based on 44″ fabric. Prepare templates, if desired, referring to drafting schematics. Cut strips and patches following schematics and chart; see *Using the Cutting Charts*, page 88. Cut binding as directed below. Except for drafting schematics, which give finished sizes, all dimensions include ¼″ seam allowance and strips include extra length, unless otherwise stated. (NOTE: Angles on all patches are either 45° or 90°.)

DIMENSIONS

FINISHED BLOCK
6″ square; about 8 ½″ diagonal

FINISHED FLAG
19″ × 13″

FINISHED WALLHANGING
23″ × 17″

MATERIALS

☐ **PINK PRINT**
¼ yd.

■ **RED PRINT**
¼ yd.

■ **BLUE PRINT**
½ yd.

BINDING
¼ yd. red solid, cut and pieced to make a 1½″ × 90″ strip.

BACKING *
¾ yd.

BATTING *

THREAD

QUILTING TEMPLATE
Single-line diamond wave, 1″ high

*Backing and batting should be cut and pieced as necessary so they are at least 4″ larger than quilt top on all sides, then trimmed to size after quilting.

DRAFTING SCHEMATICS
(No seam allowance added)

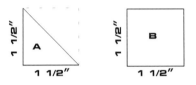

CUTTING SCHEMATICS
(Seam allowance included)

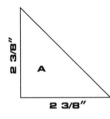

FIRST CUT			SECOND CUT			
			Number of Pieces			
Fabric and Yardage	Number of Pieces	Size	For Block	For Short Striped Field	For Long Striped Field	Size/Shape
PLAIN PATCHES						
Pink Print[1] ¼ yd.	2	1½″ × 40″	—	3	—	C 1½″ × 13½″
	2	1½″ × 40″	—	—	3	D 1½″ × 19½″
Red Print[2] ¼ yd.	2	1½″ × 40″	—	3	—	C 1½″ × 13½″
	2	1½″ × 40″	—	—	4	D 1½″ × 19½″
Blue Print[3] ½ yd.	1	2″ × 10″	4	—	—	B ■
BORDER						
	2	2½″ × 31″				
	2	2½″ × 25″				
SPEEDY TRIANGLE SQUARES[4]						
Pink Print and Blue Print[5]	1	8⅛″ × 5¾″	12	—	—	A/A ◩

[1] C's and D's are exact length. Reserve remainder of fabric for cutting triangle squares.
[2] C's and D's are exact length.
[3] Reserve remainder of fabric for cutting triangle squares.
[4] See *Speedy Triangle Squares*, page 91.
[5] Mark 3 × 2 grid of 2⅜″ squares, using remainder of fabric from plain patches and border strips.

4-Patch

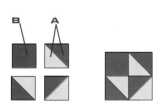

1. Arrange 3 A/A's and a B as shown. Join units to make a quarter-block. Make 4 quarter-blocks.

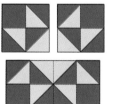

2. Join quarter-blocks, rotating as shown.

FINISHED BLOCK

Quilt Center

1. Join C's, alternating colors, to make short striped field.

2. Join D's, alternating colors, to make long striped field.

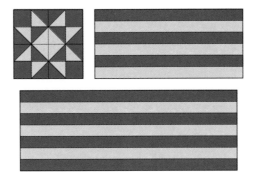

3. Arrange units as shown. Join units to make 2 rows. Join rows.

Border

Join border strips to quilt center, mitering corners.

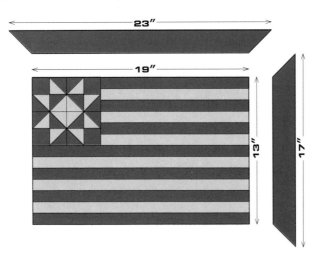

Finishing

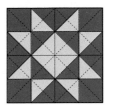

1. Mark quilting designs on quilt top.
- *For quilt block:* Mark diagonal lines across block, connecting corners of patches, to form a grid. Do not mark seams.
- *For border:* Use 1"-high single-line diamond wave template to mark a continuous design, centering it between long border edges. Mark diamond waves on each border side from the center outward, then mark identical symmetrical corners. For adjusting the length of a border design, see the *Great Cable Tip*, page 40.

2. Prepare batting and backing.

3. Assemble layers for quilting.

4. Quilt an allover grid on block, following marked lines and continuing in-the-ditch on diagonal seams. Quilt in-the-ditch around block and striped fields, and on seams between individual stripes. Quilt border design on marked lines.

5. Trim batting and backing to ½" beyond outermost seam line.

6. Bind quilt edges.

GREAT DESIGN IDEA

You can make a Little Flag crib quilt to go with the wallhanging. Double the finished size of the components and make a pair of flags. Join the flags with a 4"-wide sashing strip, add a 4"-wide border, and you will have a 46" × 64" quilt.

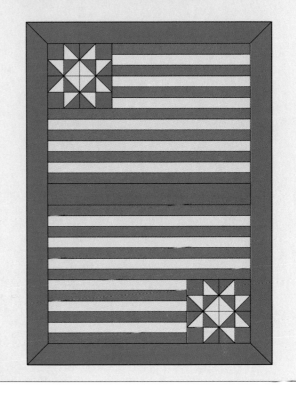

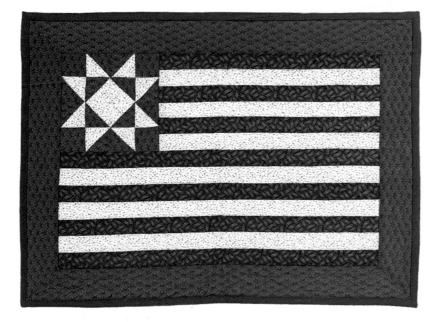

Fireworks Quilt

The pattern of this antique is apparently unique. You could find yourself imagining America as it was years ago with bandstands, picnic tables, church bazaars and the like swagged in red, white and blue bunting. Analyze the pattern and you'll see it's really an easy, but very active, pinwheel. You may want to quilt the border with the simple cable used here or let your fantasy run free with a more complex pattern.

Note: All dimensions except for binding are finished size.
Amounts for full/queen are given in parentheses.

BLOCK
20 (36) blocks, 13″ square

BORDER
4 strips, 11″ wide, cut to size,
top and bottom pieces added
before side pieces

BINDING
2″-wide strip, pieced as necessary
and cut to size.

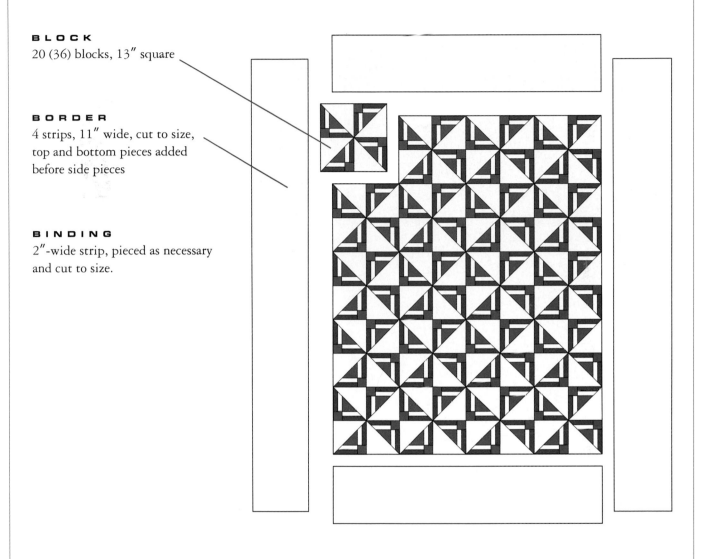

Note: Sizes and amounts for full/queen are given in parentheses.

Yardages are based on 44" fabric. Prepare templates, if desired, referring to drafting schematics. Cut strips and patches, following schematics and chart; see *Using the Cutting Charts*, page 88. Cut binding as directed below. Except for drafting schematics, which give finished sizes, all dimensions include ¼" seam allowance and all strips include extra length, unless otherwise stated. (NOTE: Unmarked angles on cutting schematics are either 45° or 90°.)

DIMENSIONS

FINISHED BLOCK
13" square; about 18⅜" diagonal

FINISHED QUILT
74" × 87" (100" square)

MATERIALS

▢ MUSLIN SOLID
8 (11¼) yds.

▣ RED SOLID
1¼ (1¾) yds.

▣ WHITE-ON-NAVY PRINT
1 (1¾) yd.

BINDING
Use ½ (¾) yd. muslin solid to make a 2" × 250" (2" × 420") strip.

BACKING *
6½ (9) yds.

BATTING *

THREAD

QUILTING TEMPLATE
4-line cable, 7" high

*Backing and batting should be cut and pieced as necessary so they are at least 4" larger than quilt top on all sides, then trimmed to size after quilting.

DRAFTING SCHEMATICS
(No seam allowance added)

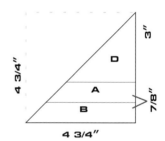

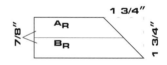

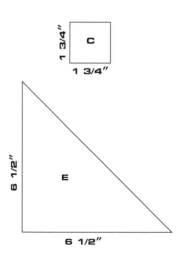

CUTTING SCHEMATICS

(Seam allowance included)

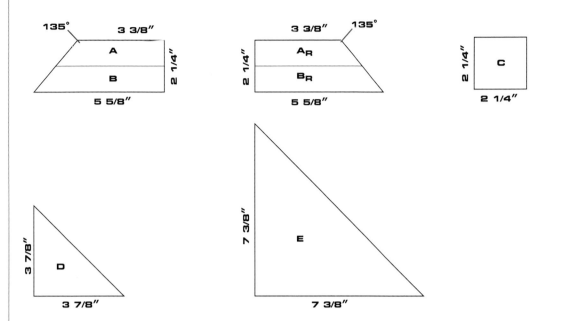

FIRST CUT			SECOND CUT	
Fabric and Yardage	Number of Pieces	Size	Number of Pieces For 20 (36) Blocks	Shape
PLAIN PATCHES				
White-on-Navy Print 1 (1¾) yd.	5 (9)	2¼″ × 40″	80 (144)	C
	4 (8)	3⅞″ × 40″	80 (144)	D
Muslin Solid 6¼ (8¾) yds.	8 (15)	7⅜″ × 40″	80 (144)	E
BORDER				
	2	11½″ × 60″ (11½″ × 86″)		
	2	11½″ × 95″ (11½″ × 108″)		

FIRST CUT			SECOND CUT	
Fabric and Yardage	Number of Pieces	Size	Method	Shape
STRIP-PIECED PATCHES*				
Muslin Solid and Red Solid 1¼ (1¾) yds. each	23 (42)	1⅜″ × 40″	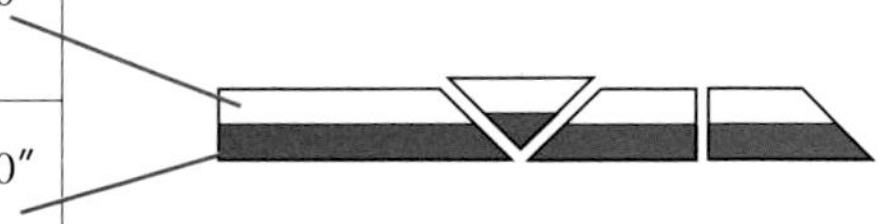	A/B
	23 (42)	1⅜″ × 40″		A_R/B_R
*Join strips lengthwise in pairs. Cut 80 (144) each of A/B and A_R/B_R.				

The size of this quilt can be adjusted easily from twin to full/queen if the number of blocks is increased to make one additional row and two additional columns. Refer to the cutting charts, page 37, for the number of pieces to cut for the different sizes.

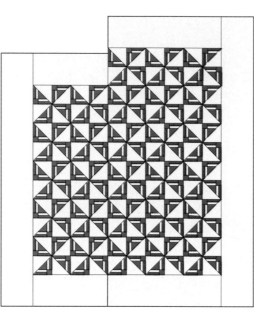

TWIN
20 blocks in a 4 × 5 layout

FULL/QUEEN
36 blocks in a 6 × 6 layout

GREAT SIZING TIP

A quick and easy way of enlarging the twin-size quilt to full/queen is to make additional borders instead of additional blocks. If you add a second and third border, both 5 1/2" wide, you will have a 96" × 109" quilt.

TWIN
1 border, 11" wide,
cut to size

FULL/QUEEN
3 borders, cut to
size: one 11" wide,
two 5 1/2" wide

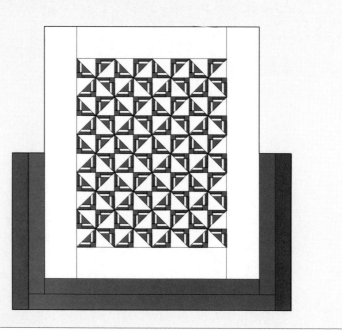

Block

Directions are given below for making one block. Amounts for making all 20 (twin) or 36 (full/queen) blocks at the same time are given in parentheses.

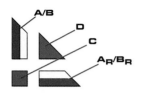

1. Arrange plain and pieced units as shown. Join units to make 2 rows. Join rows.

2. Stitch an E to piece from Step 1 to make a quarter-block. Make 4 (80) (144) quarter-blocks.

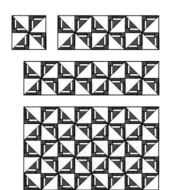

3. Join 4 quarter-blocks, rotating as shown.

FINISHED BLOCK

Quilt Center

Arrange blocks as shown. Join blocks to make rows. Join rows.

TWIN

FULL/QUEEN

Border

Join border to quilt center, shorter strips at top and bottom, then longer strips at sides.

TWIN

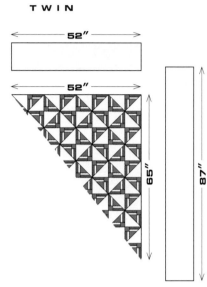

← 52″ →

← 52″ →

65″

87″

FULL/QUEEN

← 78″ →

← 78″ →

78″

100″

GREAT CABLE TIP

If you need to shorten or lengthen a cable design to fit your border, make adjustments at the center of the repeats (where they are the tallest) rather than at the ends, and connect all lines smoothly. Altering the length of a repeat may also affect its height.

You can adjust one or more cables on any number of border sides as needed. The least noticeable locations are generally the center and ends of each border side. If you find that you are adjusting a lot of cables on your quilt, you might try using a different size template.

Finishing

1. Mark quilting lines on quilt top.
- *For quilt center:* Mark an allover grid of 1⅛″ squares, making lines parallel to diagonal seams.
- *For border:* Use 7″-high 4-line cable template to mark a continuous design, centering it between long border edges. Mark cables on each border side from the center outward, then mark identical symmetrical corners. For adjusting the length of a cable design, see the *Great Cable Tip*, left.

2. Prepare batting and backing.
3. Assemble quilt layers.
4. Quilt on all marked lines.
5. Trim batting and backing to ¾″ beyond outermost seam line.
6. Bind quilt edges.

You can make a Fireworks pillow or wallhanging by changing the number and/or finished size of the components.

For a small (13"-square) pillow make a single block, or add a 1 1/2"-wide border around the block for a larger (16"-square) pillow. Quilt either size square, add a pillow back, then stuff with fiberfill. Or for the larger one, insert a 16"-square knife-edge pillow form.

PILLOWS

For a small wallhanging, make 4 blocks and arrange them in a 2 × 2 layout (26"-square). For a larger wallhanging, add one or more borders; for example, three 1 1/2"-wide borders (35" square), one 5 1/2"-wide border (39" square), or one 11"-wide border (52" square). Finish the wallhanging in the same manner as for the bed quilt, or omit the binding and display the wallhanging in a frame. For a framed project you could also replace any or all of the borders with colored mats.

WALLHANGINGS

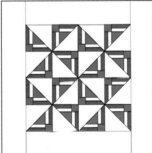

The fireworks quilt is a pinwheel pattern, and the way you place color in it will change its appearance as much as the palette you use. See what happens when you make the quarter-blocks from different colors, or make alternate blocks positive and negative. You could also make this as a scrap quilt.

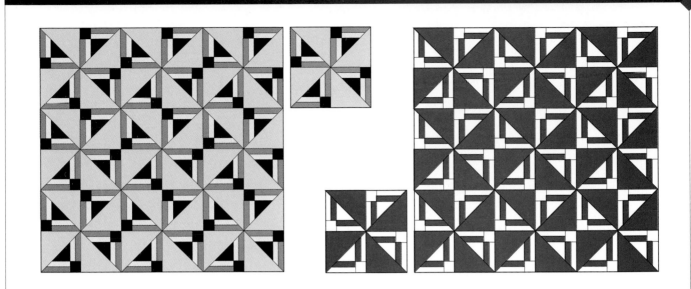
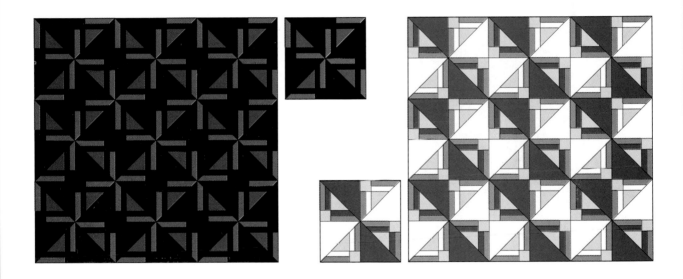

Photocopy this page, then create your own color scheme using colored pencils or markers. Refer to the examples shown, or design a unique arrangement to match your decor or please your fancy. You can create some very interesting patterns if you let a contrasting color travel diagonally from blade to blade of adjacent pinwheels.

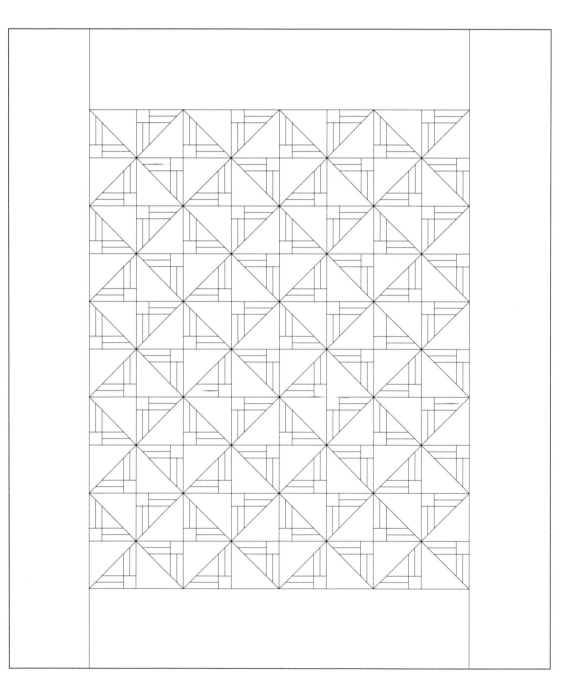

Ifyou set the Fireworks block with alternate plain blocks or sashing, the pattern will be less exuberant. If you offset the blocks by one-half block on alternate rows, or rotate the quarter-blocks before joining, you can create some altogether different geometric patterns.

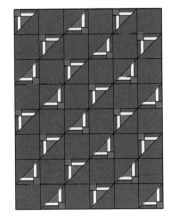

Pinwheel Star Quilt

Motion on a grand scale here, as giant stars spin in a blur of red and white and blue. Your focus shifts from the red to the white and back again, while the border width holds the movement in perfect balance. Each block mixes squares and triangles; when set together, alternate rows of white and red stars appear. This dynamic pattern is easy to reproduce as shown, or, turn to pages 56 and 57 to see how intriguingly other patterns emerge when you play with color placement in the block.

Note: All dimensions are finished size.
Amounts for full/queen are given in parentheses.

BLOCK
36 (64) blocks, 10″ square

FIRST BORDER
4 strips, 2½″ wide,
cut to size

SECOND BORDER
4 strips, 2½″ wide,
cut to size

THIRD BORDER
4 strips, 2½″ wide,
cut to size

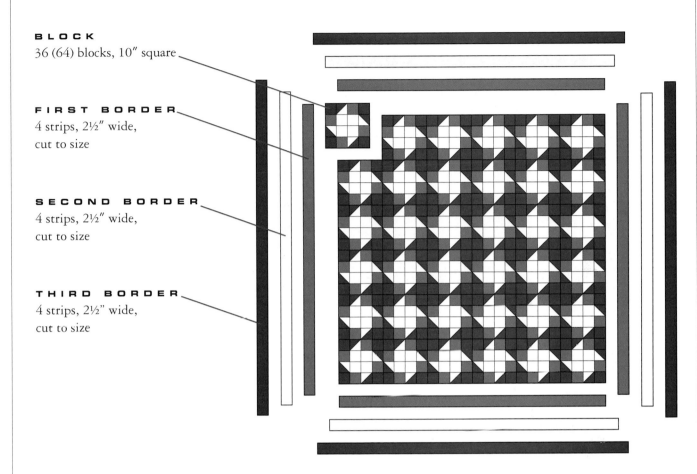

GREAT SIZING TIP

Because this pattern will repeat continuously no matter how many blocks are placed in each row or column, you can plan your quilt to be almost any size you wish. Just remember that the length of each edge will be a multiple of 10″ (one block) plus 15″ (the width of the borders).

  4 blocks in a 2 × 2 layout = 35″-square wallhanging
  9 blocks in a 3 × 3 layout = 45″-square wallhanging
  15 blocks in a 3 × 5 layout = 45″ × 65″ crib quilt

Note: Sizes and amounts for full/queen are given in parentheses.

Yardages are based on 44″ fabric. Prepare templates, if desired, referring to drafting schematics. Cut strips and patches following schematics and chart; see *Using the Cutting Charts*, page 88. Except for drafting schematics, which give finished sizes, all dimensions include ¼″ seam allowance and strips include extra length, unless otherwise stated. (NOTE: Angles on all patches are either 45° or 90°.)

DIMENSIONS

FINISHED BLOCK
10″ square; about
14½″ diagonal

FINISHED QUILT
75″ (95″) square

MATERIALS

☐ **WHITE SOLID**
2¾ (3½) yds.

☐ **MUSLIN SOLID**
2½ (3) yds.

■ **RED SOLID**
4 (5) yds.

■ **BLUE SOLID**
2½ (3) yds.

BACKING *
5 (9) yds.

BATTING *

THREAD

QUILTING TEMPLATE
2-line cable, 2″ high

*Backing and batting should be cut and pieced as necessary so they are at least 4″ larger than quilt top on all sides, then trimmed to size after quilting.

DRAFTING SCHEMATICS
(No seam allowance added)

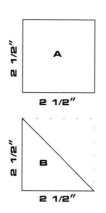

CUTTING SCHEMATICS
(Seam allowance included)

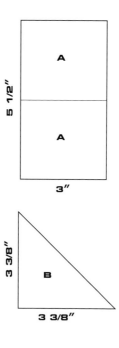

FIRST CUT			SECOND CUT	
Fabric and Yardage	Number of Pieces	Size	Number of Pieces For 36 (64) Blocks	Shape
PLAIN PATCHES				
White Solid 1¼ (1¾) yd.	12 (20)	3″ × 40″	144 (256)	A ☐
SPEEDY TRIANGLE SQUARES[1]				
White Solid 1¼ (1½) yds. and Red Solid[2]	2 (4)	21¼″ square	144 (256)	B/B ◨
FIRST BORDER				
Blue Solid[3] 2½ (3) yds.	2	3″ × 70″ (3″ × 90″)		
	2	3″ × 75″ (3″ × 95″)		
SECOND BORDER				
Muslin Solid 2½ (3) yds.	2	3″ × 75″ (3″ × 95″)		
	2	3″ × 80″ (3″ × 100″)		
THIRD BORDER				
Red Solid[4] 2½ (3) yds.	2	3″ × 80″ (3″ × 100″)		
	2	3″ × 85″ (3″ × 105″)		

[1] See *Speedy Triangle Squares*, page 91. Mark 6 × 6 grids of 3⅜″ squares.
[2] Use remainder of red solid from third border.
[3] Reserve remainder of fabric for cutting strip-pieced patches.
[4] Reserve remainder of fabric for cutting triangle squares.

FIRST CUT			SECOND CUT		
Fabric and Yardage	Number of Pieces	Size	Method	Number of Pieces	Shape
STRIP-PIECED PATCHES[1]					
Red Solid 1¼ (1¾) yds. and Blue Solid[2]	12 (20)	3″ × 40″		144 (256)	A/A
	12 (20)	3″ × 40″			

[1] Join strips lengthwise.
[2] Use remainder of blue solid from first border.

The size of this coverlet can be adjusted easily from twin to full/queen if the number of blocks is increased to make two additional rows and columns. Refer to the cutting charts, page 49, for the number of pieces to cut for the different sizes; see also the *Great Sizing Tip*, page 47.

TWIN
36 blocks in
a 6 x 6 layout

FULL/QUEEN
64 blocks in
an 8 x 8 layout

GREAT ACCESSORY IDEA

You can add one 2 1/2"-wide border to a single block to make a 15"-square pillow front. You can also rearrange the quarter-blocks to form other interesting pinwheels.

To make a pillow, first assemble the layers and quilt the pillow front, then add a pillow back and stuff with either fiberfill or a 15"-square knife-edge pillow form.

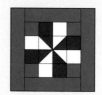

Block

Directions are given below for making one block. Amounts for making all 36 (twin) or 64 (full/queen) blocks at the same time are given in parentheses.

1. Join patches as shown to make 4 (144) (256) quarter-blocks.

2. Join 4 quarter-blocks, rotating as shown.

FINISHED BLOCK

Quilt Center

Arrange blocks as shown. Join blocks to make rows. Join rows.

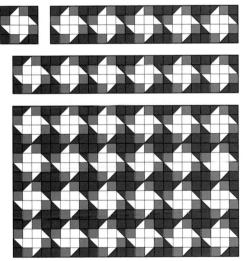

TWIN

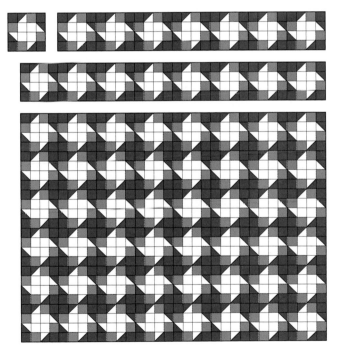

FULL/QUEEN

Borders

Join borders to quilt center, first shorter strips at top and bottom, then longer strips at sides. Complete first border before proceeding to second, then third.

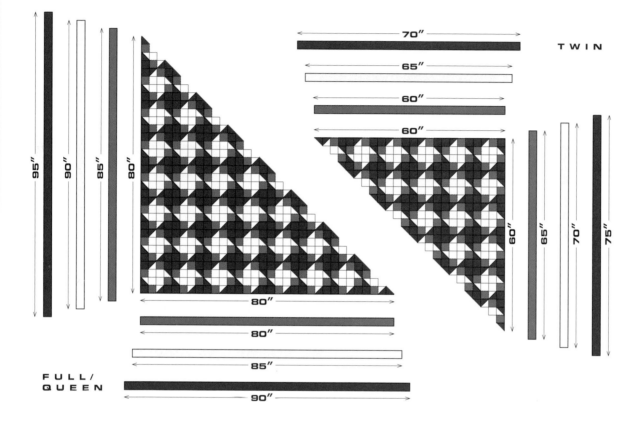

Finishing

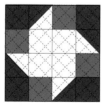

1. Mark quilting designs on quilt top.
- *For quilt center:* Mark an allover grid of 1″ squares, making lines parallel to diagonal seams. Do not mark seams.
- *For borders:* Use 2″-high 2-line cable template to mark a continuous design on each border strip, centering cables. Mark each border strip from the center outward, then mark identical symmetrical corners. (For adjusting the length of a cable design, see the *Great Cable Tip*, page 40.)

2. Prepare batting and backing.

3. Assemble quilt layers.

4. Quilt on all marked lines.

5. Trim batting even with outermost seam line. Trim quilt front and backing to ¼″ beyond batting. Bind quilt edges by pressing under ¼″ at edges of quilt top and backing, aligning folds, and slipstitching together.

A change of color can give the Pinwheel Star pattern a very different feeling. Jewel tones combined with black will make it dramatic, pastels will impart charm. Choosing prints will soften the overall pattern, while carefully cut stripes will emphasize it. Note how the pattern shifts when the placement of the colors varies from one part of the quilt to another; turn to pages 56-57 to see more examples of this.

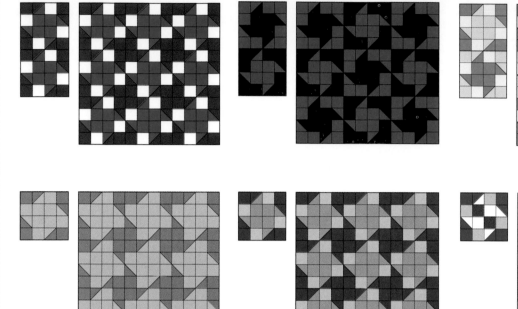

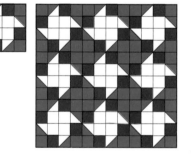

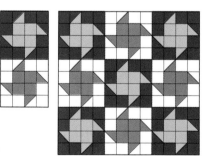

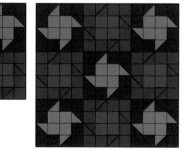

Photocopy this page, then create your own color scheme using colored pencils or markers. Refer to the examples shown, or design a unique arrangement to match your decor or please your fancy. Plan a straightforward variation of the quilt in the photographs, or experiment with the tessellation to find new patterns.

Graphic designs that make interlocking patterns when they repeat are known as tessellations. Often, the unit that repeats is not terribly interesting on its own. If, for instance, you change the set of the Pinwheel Star block by adding plain blocks or sashing it will lose its impact. However, when you insert sashing between four-block units, you see the pattern again.

Tessellating designs are fascinating. When the colors or color values used in them are rearranged, the viewer sees an illusion of a change in the design itself. Here are six examples of how the Pinwheel Star pattern can be altered by the arrangement of color.

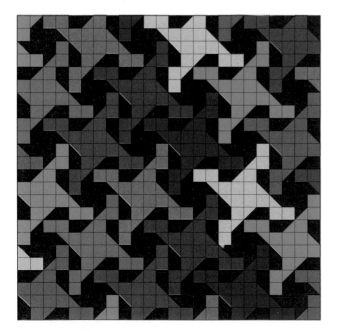 

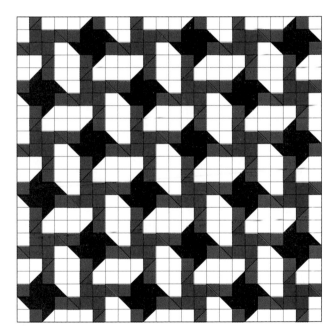

Standing Star Quilt

BY KATHARINE BRAINARD

When commissioned to create a Stars and Stripes quilt, Katharine wanted it to be "something new, yet something you'd seen a million times before." You'll find her block is simple and graphic but the effect is very exciting when you repeat it. Faded colors contrast with bold, clean lines and get you right into the heart of the American experience.

Note: All dimensions except for binding are finished size. The outermost repeat of the zigzag border is slightly irregular; the one on the top and bottom differs from that on the sides, both differ from all the central zigzags. If you follow the schematics and directions to cut and piece the correct units, your borders will fit as shown in the drawings.

PLAIN CORNER SQUARE
20 plain 1″ corner squares

PIECED CORNER SQUARE
4 pieced 4″ corner squares

BINDING
1¼″ wide strip pieced as necessary and cut to size

BLOCK
12 blocks, 8″ square

SASHING
31 sashing strips, 1″ × 8″

FIRST BORDER
4 plain border strips, ½″ wide

SECOND BORDER
4 pieced border strips, 4″ wide

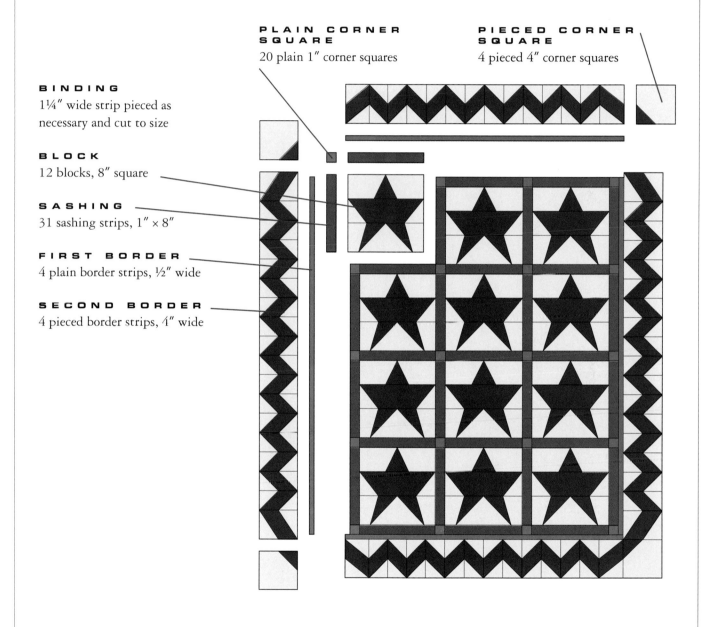

Yardages are based on 44″ fabric. Prepare templates, if desired, referring to drafting schematics. Actual-size patterns for the star are on pages 95 and 96. Cut strips and patches following schematics and charts; see *Using the Cutting Charts*, page 88. Cut binding as directed below. Except for drafting schematics, which give finished sizes, all dimensions include ¼″ seam allowance and strips include extra length, unless otherwise stated. (NOTE: Unmarked angles on cutting schematics are either 45° or 90°.)

DIMENSIONS

FINISHED BLOCK
8″ square; about 11⅜″ diagonal

FINISHED QUILT
37″ × 46″

MATERIALS

□ **MUSLIN SOLID**
3 yds.

■ **RED SOLID**
2¼ yds.

■ **RED/WHITE STRIPE**
½ yd.

■ **BLUE SOLID**
1¾ yds.

BINDING
Use ½ yd. blue solid to cut and piece a 1¼″ × 190″ strip.

BACKING *
3 yds.

BATTING *

THREAD

*Backing and batting should be cut and pieced as necessary so they are at least 4" larger than quilt top on all sides, then trimmed to size after quilting.

DRAFTING SCHEMATICS

(No seam allowance added. Turn templates over to mark or cut reverse pieces.)

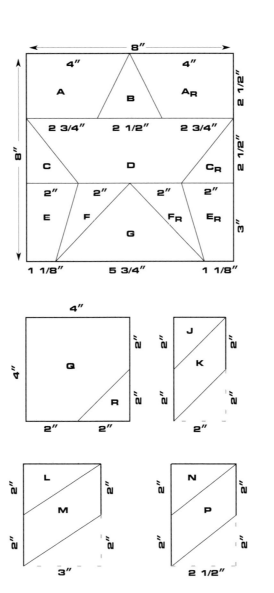

CUTTING SCHEMATICS

(Seam allowance included. Actual-size patterns for pieces A through G are on pages 95 and 96).

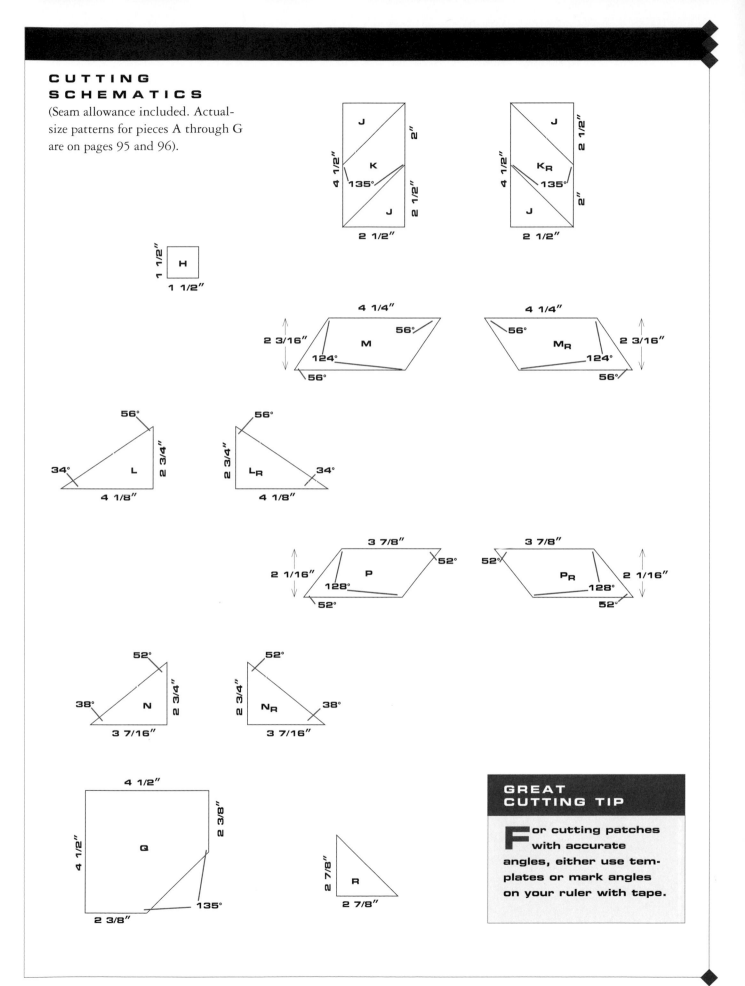

GREAT CUTTING TIP

For cutting patches with accurate angles, either use templates or mark angles on your ruler with tape.

FIRST CUT			SECOND CUT		
			Number of Pieces		
Fabric and Yardage	Number of Pieces	Size	For 12 Blocks	For Second Border	Shape
PLAIN PATCHES*					
Muslin Solid 1¼ yds.	3	3″ × 40″	12	—	A
			12	—	A$_R$
	1	3½″ × 40″	12	—	C
			12	—	C$_R$
	2	3½″ × 40″	12	—	E
			12	—	E$_R$
	1	2¾″ × 20″	—	4	L
			—	4	L$_R$
	1	2¾″ × 20″	—	4	N
			—	4	N$_R$
	2	3⅝″ × 40″	4	—	G
	1	4½″ × 40″	—	4	Q
Red Solid 1 yd.	1	3¼″ × 40″	12	—	B
	3	3″ × 40″	12	—	D
	4	2″ × 40″	12	—	F
			12	—	F$_R$
	1	2³/₁₆″ × 40″	—	2	M
			—	2	M$_R$
	1	2¹/₁₆″ × 40″	—	2	P
			—	2	P$_R$
	1	2⅞″ × 20″	—	4	R

*Cut mirror image pieces from same strips.

FIRST CUT			SECOND CUT	
Fabric and Yardage	Number of Pieces	Size	Number of Pieces	Size/Shape
SASHING				
Red/White Stripe ½ yd.	8	1½″ × 40″	31	1½″ × 8½″ (exact length)
Blue Solid*	1	1½″ × 40″	20	H 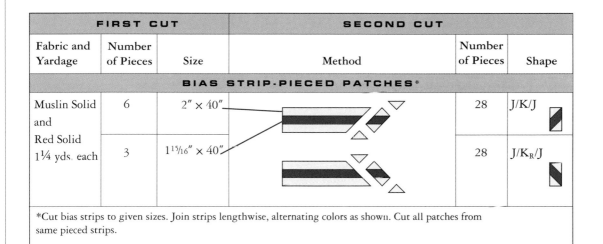
FIRST BORDER				
Blue Solid* 1¼ yds.	2	1″ × 35″		
	2	1″ × 43″		
*Cut H's from remainder of fabric from first border.				

FIRST CUT			SECOND CUT		
Fabric and Yardage	Number of Pieces	Size	Method	Number of Pieces	Shape
BIAS STRIP-PIECED PATCHES*					
Muslin Solid and Red Solid 1¼ yds. each	6	2″ × 40″		28	J/K/J
	3	1¹⁵⁄₁₆″ × 40″		28	J/K_R/J
*Cut bias strips to given sizes. Join strips lengthwise, alternating colors as shown. Cut all patches from same pieced strips.					

GREAT SIZING TIP

Those of you who have fallen in love with this jaunty pieced star might consider making it up as a bed quilt. Because the border repeat is somewhat irregular, it can be tricky to change the size of this quilt by adding blocks. An easier way is to double the finished size of the components (enlarge them to 200%). This makes a 74″ × 92″ twin coverlet. You will need about four times as much fabric for the large quilt as for the small one.

Block

Arrange patches as shown. Join patches to make 3 rows. Join rows. Make 12 blocks.

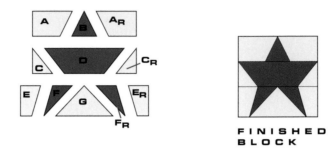

FINISHED
BLOCK

Quilt Center

Arrange units as shown. Join units to make rows. Join rows.

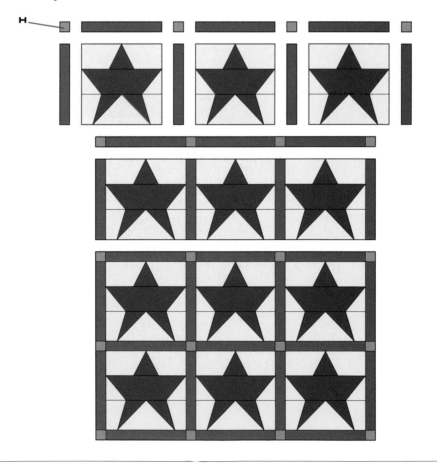

First Border

Join border strips to quilt center, first longer strips at sides, then shorter strips at top and bottom.

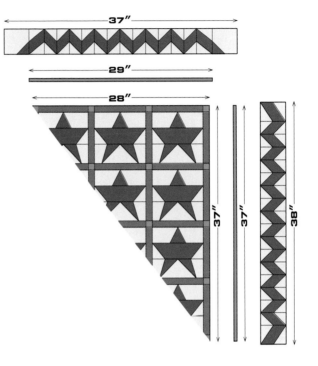

Second Border

1. Stitch L, M, L and L_R, M_R, L_R pieces together as shown to make 2 L/M/L and 2 $L_R/M_R/L_R$ units.

2. Join 8 J/K/J, 8 $J/K_R/J$, one L/M/L, and one $L_R/M_R/L_R$ unit as shown to make 2 side border strips. Join strips to quilt sides.

3. Stitch N, P, N and N_R, P_R, N_R pieces together as shown to make 2 N/P/N and 2 $N_R/P_R/N_R$ units.

4. Join Q and R to make 4 pieced corner squares.

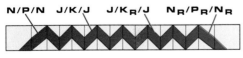

5. Join 6 J/K/J, 6 $J/K_R/J$, one N/P/N, one $N_R/P_R/N_R$, and 2 Q/R units as shown to make top and bottom border strips. Join strips to quilt top.

Finishing

1. Prepare batting and backing.
2. Assemble quilt layers.
3. Quilt in-the-ditch around red stars and on inner and outer seams of red border design. Echo-quilt outward from red shapes on muslin patches, making lines of quilting ½″ apart.
4. Trim batting and backing to ⅜″ beyond outermost seam line.
5. Bind quilt edges.

GREAT QUICK IDEA

You can use leftovers from the quilt to make a 10″-square potholder. Use polyester batting only if the pot-holder will be a decorative item, because polyester is a conductor of heat. For your potholder to be utilitarian, use cotton batting to provide the needed insulation.

First make a single block and frame it with sashing and corner squares as for the quilt.

Next assemble the quilt layers. Quilt in-the-ditch on all sashing seams and around the red star. Echo-quilt around the star.

Finally, bind the potholder and add a hanging loop.

You can make a 19"-square pillow to match the Standing Star quilt, using 1 yd. muslin solid, 3/4 yd. red solid, 1/2 yd. blue solid, 1/4 yd. red/white stripe, and 3/4 yd. each of lining and backing. You will also need polyester fiberfill for stuffing and 2 1/4 yds. of 1/8"-diameter cording.

Make the pillow front in a similar manner as for the quilt, except substituting S/T/U and V/W/Y units for L/M/L, N/P/N, and Q/R units; see the schematics below.

When the pillow front is complete, assemble the layers and quilt them. Add a pillow back and covered cording all around the edges. Stuff the pillow firmly with fiberfill.

DRAFTING SCHEMATIC
(No seam allowance added. Turn templates over to mark or cut reversed pieces.)

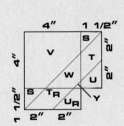

CUTTING SCHEMATICS
(Seam allowance included.)

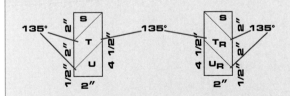

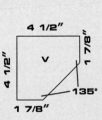

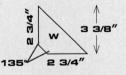

For other all-American versions of this bold pattern, try blue or white stars on red or blue backgrounds—you could even set up a checkerboard pattern. The whimscal appeal of this pattern lends itself to childlike pastels or primitive earth tones, and it would be very striking in jewel tones on a dark ground. The sashing fabric need not be a stripe—why not use a celestial print?

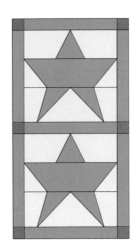
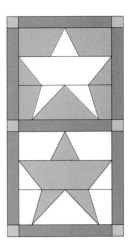

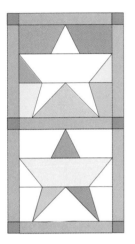
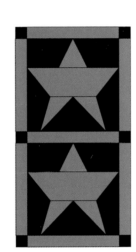
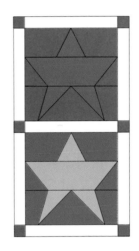
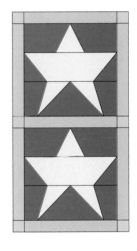

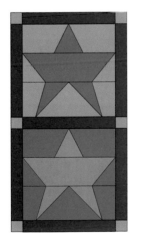
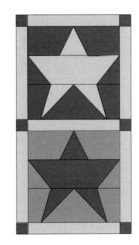
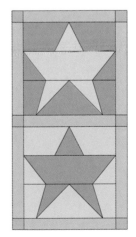
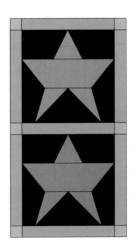

Photocopy this page, then create your own color scheme using colored pencils or markers. Refer to the examples shown, or design a unique arrangement to match your decor or please your fancy. Note how different the pattern looks if the plain squares match, rather than contrast, the background.

This star block is too strongly one-directional to be successful set on point. You could set it with alternate plain blocks, with or without sashing. If you omit the sashing, you can rotate adjacent blocks to create unexpected patterns. Omitting the sashing will change the quilt size; recalculate the zigzag border if you wish to use it.

Patriotic Stars Wallhanging

BY DIANE RODE SCHNECK

Tradition and patriotism shine brightly in an eloquent new take on Old Glory. This gifted, longtime quilter miniaturized a block she created to commemorate the Persian Gulf War (turn to the Expert's Challenge to see the original in a sampler quilt created by her quilters' computer group). Using her scraps for inspiration, Diane pieced the flag into the multi-red Evening Stars, then penned a message on the appliquéd center star. This is an interesting project that is easy enough to piece in a weekend.

Note: All dimensions except for binding are finished size.

BORDER

4 strips, 3″ wide, cut to size (top and bottom pieces added before side pieces)

BINDING

1″-wide strip, pieced as necessary and cut to size

FLAG BLOCK

8 blocks, 6″ square

STAR BLOCK

1 block, 6″ square

CORNER SQUARE

4 corner squares, 3″ square

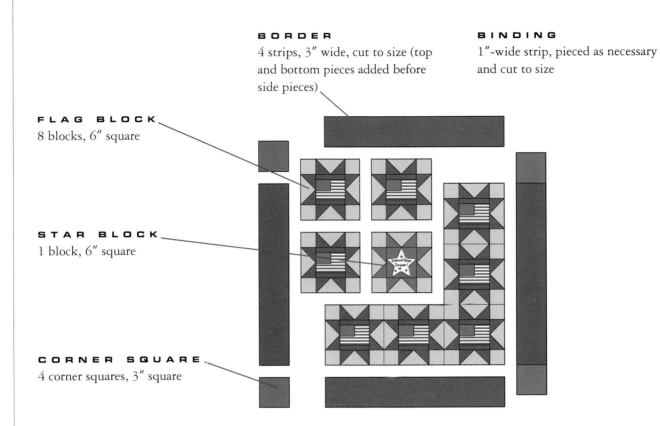

GREAT APPLIQUÉ TIP

To make crisp edges and sharp points on a star, first clip into the seam allowance at the inner corners, cutting just up to but not through the seam line. Fold the seam allowance at each point to the wrong side. Press.

Then press under the seam allowance on both sides of the point. Trim away any seam allowance that extends outside the folds.

Yardages are based on 44" fabric. Prepare templates for patches and star field appliqué, if desired, referring to drafting schematics. Prepare actual-size star pattern, page 77, for hand-appliqué, adding ¼" seam allowance. Cut strips, patches, and appliqués following schematics and chart; see *Using the Cutting Charts*, page 88. Cut binding as directed below. Except for drafting schematics, which give finished sizes, all dimensions include ¼" seam allowance and strips include extra length, unless otherwise stated. (NOTE: Angles on all patches are either 45° or 90°.)

DIMENSIONS

FINISHED FLAG BLOCK
6" square; about
8½" diagonal

FINISHED STAR BLOCK
6" square; about
8½" diagonal

FINISHED QUILT
24" square

GREAT FABRIC TIP

This little quilt is a wonderful scrap project. 1/4 yard quantities are listed since that is often the smallest cut a store will make, but you may find all the fabric you need in your scrap collection.

MATERIALS

MUSLIN TEA DYED PRINT
½ yd.

MUSLIN SOLID
¼ yd.

RED/WHITE STRIPE
¼ yd.

RED/BLACK CHECK
¼ yd.

ASSORTED RED PRINTS (8)
¼ yd. each

NAVY PRINT
¼ yd.

BINDING
½ yd. navy denim-look print, cut and pieced to make a 1" × 110" strip.

BACKING＊
¾ yd.

BATTING＊

THREAD

*Backing and batting should be cut and pieced as necessary so they are at least 4" larger than quilt top on all sides, then trimmed to size after quilting.

DRAFTING SCHEMATICS

(No seam allowance added)

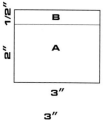

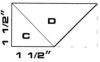

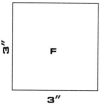

FIRST CUT			SECOND CUT			
			Number of Pieces			
Fabric and Yardage	Number of Pieces	Size	For 8 Flag Blocks	For 1 Star Block	For 4 Corner Squares	Shape
PATCHES						
Red/White Stripe ¼ yd.	1	3½" × 40"	8	—	—	A 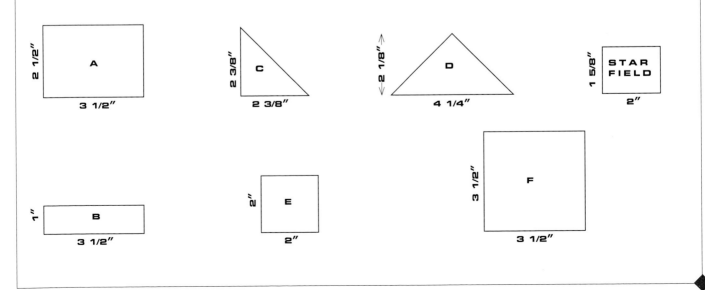
Assorted Red Prints[1] ¼ yd.	2	1" × 40"	16	—	—	B
	2	2⅜" × 40"	64	—	—	C
Navy Print[2] ¼ yd.	1	2⅜" × 40"	—	8	—	C
	1	3½" × 40"	—	1	4	F
Muslin Tea Dyed Print ½ yd.	2	2⅛" × 40"	32	4	—	D
	2	2" × 40"	32	4	—	E
APPLIQUÉS						
Navy Print[3]	1	1⅝" × 40"	8	—	—	Star Field
Muslin Solid ¼ yd.	1	—	—	1	—	Star
BORDER						
Red/Black Check ¼ yd.	4	3½" × 40"				

[1]Cut 2 A's and 8 C's from each of 8 different prints.
[2]Reserve remainder of fabric for cutting appliqués.
[3]Use remainder of fabric from patches.

CUTTING SCHEMATICS

(Seam allowance included)

Flag Block

Directions are given below for making one block. Amounts for making all 8 blocks at the same time are given in parentheses.

1. Press under seam allowance at one long edge and one short edge of one (8) star field appliqué. Baste star field on one (8) A, aligning raw edges. Hand-appliqué star field in place at pressed edges.

2. Join 2 B's to one (8) A.

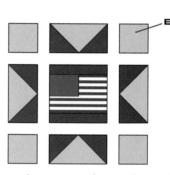

3. Sew 2 red C's to 4 (32) D's.

4. Arrange patches as shown. Join patches to make 3 rows. Join rows.

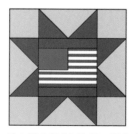

FINISHED FLAG BLOCK

Star Block

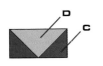

1. Sew 2 blue C's to 4 D's.

2. Use actual-size star pattern, below, to mark lettering and designs on star appliqué with a brown fine-point permanent marking pen.

3. Press under seam allowance at all edges of star appliqué; see the *Great Appliqué Tip*, page 73. Baste star on F, centered. Hand-appliqué star in place.

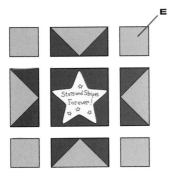

4. Arrange and join patches in same manner as for Flag Block, Step 4.

FINISHED STAR BLOCK

ACTUAL-SIZE PATTERN

Quilt Center

Arrange blocks as shown. Join blocks to make 3 rows. Join rows.

Border

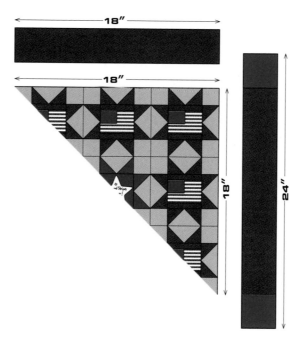

1. Join corner squares to side border strips.

2. Join border to quilt center, first plain strips at top and bottom, then pieced strips at sides.

Finishing

1. Mark quilting designs on quilt top.

♦ *For corner squares:* Use actual-size pattern, page 77, to mark a star.

♦ *For border strips:* Mark parallel lines 1½″ apart, perpendicular to long edges.

2. Prepare batting and backing.

3. Assemble layers for quilting.

4. Quilt on marked lines. Quilt in-the-ditch around appliquéd star and red pieced stars.

5. Trim batting and backing to ¼″ beyond outermost seam line.

6. Bind quilt edges.

GREAT SIZING IDEA

If you consider the quilt center as a single 9-patch block, you can make and join a number of such blocks to form a larger quilt. You can frame the blocks with 3″-wide sashing and corner squares, then finish with a matching border, and because the pattern will repeat continuously, you can plan your quilt to be almost any size you wish. Just remember that the length of each edge will be a multiple of 18″ (one block) plus a multiple of 3″ (sashing and border width). Some examples:

6 blocks in a 2 × 3 layout = 45″ × 66″ crib quilt

16 blocks in a 4 × 4 layout = 87″-square twin quilt

25 blocks in a 5 × 5 layout = 108″-square full/queen quilt

Featuring the American flag as it does, this pattern really ought to remain red-white-and-blue. However, you could change the relative positions of the colors, or choose other hues. Of course, if you omit the flag and make the star center from a plain square, you will have a traditional Evening Star block that can be colored any way you like.

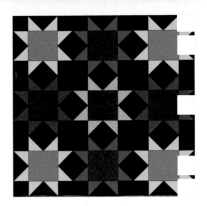

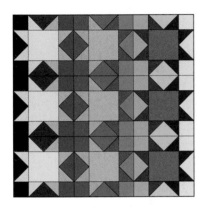
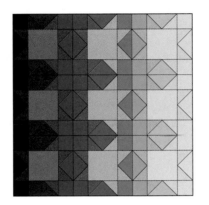
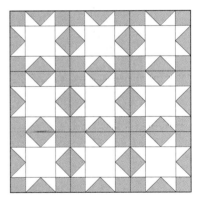

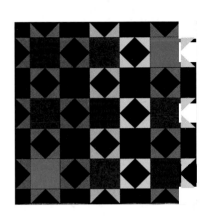

Photocopy this page, then create your own color scheme using colored pencils or markers. Refer to the examples shown, or design a unique arrangement to match your decor or please your fancy. Note how the background pattern changes in importance when you change the balance of dark and light colors.

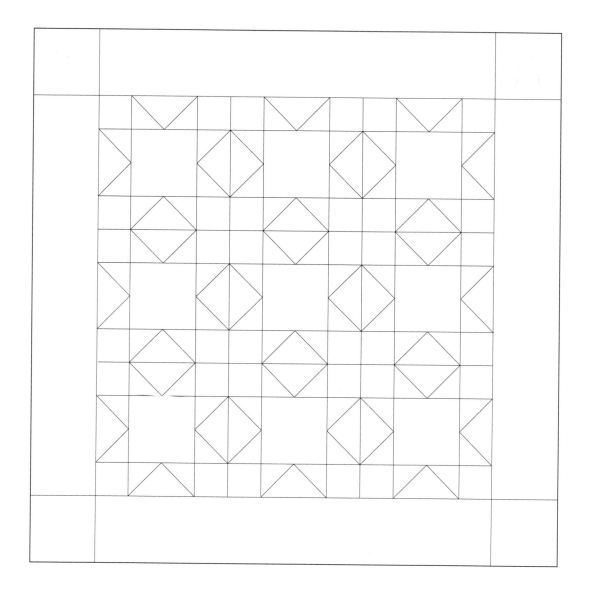

To create variations of this patriotic wallhanging, you can easily arrange eight star blocks around a single flag block, or alternate the two. You could also add sashing between the blocks, which will make the quilt a little larger. If you use only star-centered blocks, or make the blocks with plain centers, you can turn them on point.

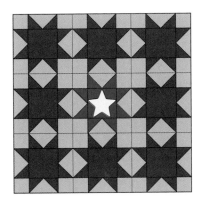

Stars and Stripes Forever

BY DIANE RODE SCHNECK
AND MEMBERS OF ONLINE QUILTERS,
CHAPTER TWO

Stars and stripes fill this sampler, which was made during the Persian Gulf War. Blocks were created and exchanged by 25 members of an online computer group, then each one assembled her vision of a patriotic quilt. You and your fellow quilters might want to create a sampler with the blocks used in this book; see page 87.

By Anne Lucietto of Yorkville, Illinois.

Judy Cohen of Los Angeles, California, made this block from a design by Judy Martin.

By Elaine Solomon of Lexington, Kentucky, who adapted this design from one by Georgia Bonesteel.

QUILTMAKING TRADITIONS

Quilters live in their times. They have opinions, take stands, often express their thoughts and feelings in their quilts. This is a long and honored tradition.

Many a pioneer cabin held a going-away quilt, made to send best wishes for a new life from those left behind. Favorite recipients of commemorative or thank you quilts were ministers being transferred, teachers moving on or up, honored town leaders. One of the Online quilts was given to the Commander of Desert Storm, General Norman A. Schwartzkopf. Births and birthdays, life histories, hobbies and work all engaged quilters as proper themes for their bed covers and wall hangings. Quilts were made to raise money for the church, school — and during the Wars, Civil and World War I — to raise money for medicines and supplies for the troops.

While today's vibrant, active quilters often struggle to overcome the image of 'little old ladies in the parlor', they continue to express their concerns, pleasures and delights in the medium of fabric and thread. The Expert's Challenge Quilt we show is very much a quilt of the Nineties in its choice of subject, and yet it partakes of the tradition of community in its making.

The community responsible for this sampler quilt is no small town quilt guild. It is a national, computer linked group of quilters who trade ideas, blocks, and passions daily via a computer network. Simply a new definition of community meeting, sharing and quilting on the information super highway.

Early in the fall of 1990, Jody McFadden of Sacramento, California proposed to her fellow Online Quilters a red, white and blue fabric swap and 25 of the group signed on. As the swap was organized, members began to discuss how they felt about the chances of an incident in the Persian Gulf, about the possibility of war and how it would affect them and the country, their ideas of patriotism and their interpretation of the Constitution. At the same time, each one of the 25 quilters chose one fabric and sent it along to the other 24. All the quilters worked with the same selection of fabrics. Each quilter pieced 25 blocks of her own design, sent them off and in turn received 24 pieced by the others. Each quilter assembled her own quilt, arranging the 25 blocks, with or without sashing, designed a patriotic backing and finally quilted the whole.

THOUGHTS FROM THE QUILTER

We heard about the patriotic sampler quilts through Diane Rode Schneck, an Online Quilter, whose version is our Expert's Challenge. Diane, who contributed the Patriotic Star block (see the wallhanging on page 72), recalls, "I appreciated being involved in a group activity during this very uncertain time. What I did discover was a real love affair with the Stars and Stripes. I must have bought every star-printed fabric on the market."

By Norma McKone of Silver Spring, Maryland.

By Ellen Crockett of Springfield, Virginia.

Diane complemented this star print with a quilted star-in-star.

By Louise Geesaman of Jenkintown, Pennsylvania.

We offer you this challenge quilt as an inspiration. The drawing below shows one way you could use the blocks from the quilts in this book as the basis for a patriotic sampler quilt. Mix them with other blocks—as shown or as you wish—and fill any irregular spaces with sashing.

You may or may not be a member of an active quilt guild. You may want to join one, or start one. Take up the challenge. Quilt up a storm.

Appendix

USING THE CUTTING CHARTS

The sample cutting charts and schematics below demonstrate how these elements work together to provide the information needed to cut most of the pieces for any quilt project in the Better Homes and Gardens® Creative Quilting Collection volumes. Any additional cuts, such as for binding, can be found in the Fabric and Cutting List for each project.

DRAFTING SCHEMATIC ——————

Drafting schematics, which do not include seam allowance, are provided for your convenience as an aid in preparing templates.

DRAFTING SCHEMATIC
(No seam allowance added)

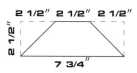

CUTTING SCHEMATIC ——————

Cutting schematics, which do include seam allowance, can be used for preparing templates (with seam allowance included) but are given primarily as an aid for speed-cutting shapes using a rotary cutter and special rulers with angles marked on them.

CUTTING SCHEMATICS
(Seam allowance included)

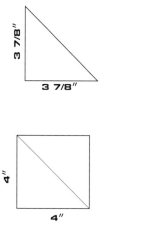

FABRIC AND YARDAGE
This column gives the color and amount of fabric needed to cut groups of shapes, rounded up to the next ¼ yard. To change the color scheme of a project, refer to the dimensions given for individual groups of shapes and use (combine them as needed) to calculate the new yardage.

FIRST CUT
Cut the number of pieces in the sizes indicated on either the lengthwise or crosswise grain unless otherwise stated, using templates or rotary cutting rulers. For 40″-long strips, cutting completely across the width of the fabric usually provides the most economical cuts.

SECOND CUT
Cut the number of pieces in the sizes and/or shapes indicated, referring to the cutting schematics for angles and cut sizes. Reversed pieces are designated by a subscript $_R$ (e.g., the reverse of a B patch is designated B_R) and can frequently be obtained from the same strips as their mirror images by cutting the two shapes alternately.

BORDER
From ½ yd. blue check cut two 2½″ × 29″ and two 2½″ × 32″ border strips.

FOOTNOTE
Use the cited instructions for Speedy Triangle Squares and mark the grids in the layout indicated.

APPLIQUÉS
From ¼ yd. red floral cut 16 flowers and 8 buds. From ¼ yd. blue floral cut 56 leaves. Reversed pieces are designated by a subscript $_R$ and these patterns should be turned over before marking onto fabric.

8 RED SOLID A'S
From ¼ yd. red solid, cut one 3⅞″ × 20″ strip. From strip cut four 3⅞″ squares. Cut squares in half to make 8 right-triangle A's.

6 WHITE SOLID C'S
From ¼ yd. white solid cut one 3½″ × 40″ strip. From strip cut six trapezoids.

FOOTNOTE REFERENCE
See the footnote underneath the chart for additional information about cutting this group of shapes.

	FIRST CUT		SECOND CUT	
Fabric and Yardage	Number of Pieces	Size	Number of Pieces	Shape
PLAIN PATCHES				
Red Solid ¼ yd.	1	3⅞″ × 20″	8	A
	1	3½″ × 40″	8	B
White Solid ¼ yd.	1	3⅞″ × 20″	8	A
	1	3½″ × 40″	6	C
SPEEDY TRIANGLE SQUARES				
Red Solid and White Solid ½ yd. each	2	16½″ × 20⅝″	72	B/B[1]
BORDER				
Blue Check ½ yd.	2	2½″ × 29″		
	2	2½″ × 32″		

[1] See *Speedy Triangle Squares* (page 93). Mark 4 × 5 grids with 3⅞″ squares.

APPLIQUÉS		
Fabric and Yardage	Number of Pieces	Shape
Red Floral ¼ yd.	16	Flower
	8	Bud
Blue Floral ¼ yd.	56	Leaf

Refer as well to Great Quiltmaking: All the Basics, *the detailed companion to the volumes in the* Better Homes and Gardens® *Creative Quilting Collection.*

Preparing to Cut

Plan the cuts before beginning. Fabric for the largest pieces, such as borders, should be marked first, then the smaller pieces for patchwork. (NOTE: Allow extra length for border pieces in case the actual quilt measurements differ from the planned size.)

BORDERS		
BIAS STRIPS	LARGE PIECES	SMALL PIECES

Placement on the Fabric Grain

Cut the pieces with one or more long edges on the straight grain, parallel to the fabric threads. Cut as many pieces as possible on the crosswise grain to conserve fabric. Cut long pieces on the lengthwise grain to minimize piecing.

Cutting Bias Strips

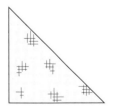

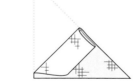

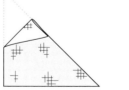

1. Cut a fabric square in half diagonally (along the bias).

2. Beginning at one 45° corner, fold fabric repeatedly, aligning bias edges.

3. Cut strips parallel to bias edge.
4. Join strip ends to make a longer strip.

Speedy Triangle Squares

1. Cut matching pieces of two contrasting fabrics (see individual project directions for dimensions).

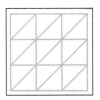 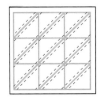

2. Mark a square grid on wrong side of lighter-color fabric, leaving ½″ margin all around grid. Mark half as many grid squares as triangle squares needed; each marked square will make two pieced squares. (NOTE: Mark grid squares ⅞″ larger than desired finished size of triangle squares.)

3. Mark diagonals across squares.

4. Pin marked fabric to contrasting fabric, right sides together. Stitch ¼″ from each diagonal, on both sides of line.

5. Cut along marked lines, grid lines first and then diagonals.

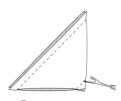

6. Remove corner stitches.

7. Open triangles. Press seams toward darker fabric.

Successful Seams

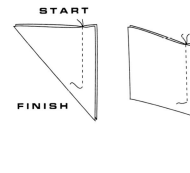

START

FINISH

◆ *Sewing acute angles (less than 90°):* Start at end with larger corner angle and stitch across piece to end with acute angle. (NOTE: Stitching into seam allowance is not advisable at acute angles. Unless the seam allowance is left free, it may be difficult to align adjacent edges that have not yet been stitched.)

 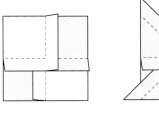 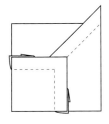

◆ *For seams pressed toward lighter fabric:* Trim darker seam allowance to ⅛″, to prevent it from extending beyond lighter seam allowance and showing through on right side.

◆ *For intersections of seams:* Press seams away from each other, either open or to one side. (NOTE: At intersections of four or more pieces, press all seams either clockwise or counterclockwise.)

◆ *For set-in seams:* Press the joining seam(s) of the outer pieces to one side. Press seam allowances of the set-in piece flat, toward the outer pieces.

Simple Continuous Binding

1. Press under seam allowance on one long edge and one end of binding strip.

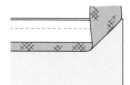
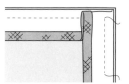

2. Pin and stitch binding strip to quilt top, aligning seam lines, beginning at center of one quilt edge with folded end of strip and stopping at seam line of next quilt edge; break threads.

3. To miter corner, press strip away from quilt on a 45° angle, then press it back over quilt. Stitch, beginning at end of previous stitching line (a tuck will form at corner). At beginning point, trim binding and lap ends 1″; stitch.

4. Fold binding over corners to backing, forming miters at tucks. Position long folded edge of binding over seam line, forming miters at corners. Slipstitch, stitching into miters to secure.

Individual Binding Strips

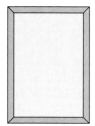
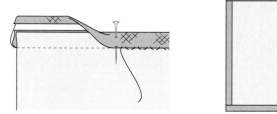

1. Prepare simple binding.
- **For mitered corners:** Stitch binding strips to quilt top, making machine-stitched mitered corners (see Chapter 3, "The Quilt Components"). Fold binding over quilt edges to backing; pin, making neat mitered or butted corners.

- **For butted corners:** Stitch one pair of binding strips to opposite edges of quilt top. Trim ends even with quilt. Fold strips to backing; slipstitch. Apply second pair of strips to remaining quilt edges in same manner, folding ends under instead of trimming.

Binding strip length = Length of quilt edge + 1″

French Fold Binding

French fold binding is made the same way as other separate, continuous bindings but uses more fabric because it is applied doubled.

Binding strip width = (Binding width x 4) + ½″
Binding strip length = Perimeter of quilt + 1″

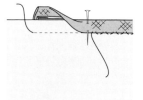

1. Press under ¼″ at one end of binding strip. Press strip in half lengthwise, right side out.
2. Apply folded binding as for other bindings: Place raw edges of binding toward raw edge of quilt. It will not be necessary to press under free edge of binding as it is already folded.

Hanging a Quilt with Rings

Lightweight plastic rings (available in crafts shops and hardware stores) provide a simple way to hang a quilt. For a small wallhanging (up to about 20″ square), three ½″diameter rings should be sufficient. For a larger project, buy enough rings so that they can be spaced 7″ to 9″ apart along the top edge of the quilt. You will need to affix one small nail (or picture hook) in the wall to support each plastic ring.

1. Position one ring on backing, centered and 1″ below top edge. Sew center bottom of ring in place securely with a few hand-stitches, making sure stitches don't show through on front of quilt.

2. Stitch a ring to each end of backing top, 1″ from top and side edges.

3. Space any additional rings evenly between those already stitched in place.

4. To mount quilt, place rings over nails (or picture hooks) on wall.

Hanging a Quilt with a Sleeve

A fabric sleeve can be sewn to the quilt backing for holding a wooden dowel or lattice strip that will support the weight of the quilt evenly and completely across the top. The larger and heavier the quilt, the sturdier the dowel or lattice strip must be.

The ends of the dowel or lattice strip can extend beyond the quilt sides and be capped with decorative finials, or they can stop just short of the sides and support the quilt invisibly.

Dowels can be supported with appropriate sizes of finishing (headless) nails, cup hooks, or small brackets. If using nails, be sure they extend sufficiently from the wall to hold the dowel.

MAKING A SLEEVE

1. Cut a 3″-wide fabric strip 2½″ shorter than width of quilt. (NOTE: If the quilt is very wide or heavy, make several shorter sleeves that will be spaced evenly across the quilt so the dowel can be affixed to supporting nails in several places.)

2. Press under ¼″ on each edge of strip. Topstitch fold allowance at ends.

3. Center strip (sleeve) across quilt backing ½″ below top edge; pin.

4. Hand-stitch long edges of sleeve securely to quilt backing, making sure stitches don't show through on front of quilt. Do not stitch ends.

1. Cut dowel (or lattice strip) 1″ shorter than quilt width. If supporting with nails, drill a small hole ¼″ in from each end.

2. Seal wood with polyurethane to prevent wood seepage from discoloring fabric. Let dry thoroughly. (NOTE: Follow manufacturer's directions for method of application and drying time.)

♦ *If using nails to support quilt:* Measure, mark, and affix them to wall the same distance apart as holes in wood.

♦ *If using brackets or cup hooks to support quilt:* Measure, mark, and affix to wall appropriately.

3. Slide dowel (or lattice strip) through fabric sleeve, centering it between quilt sides so that holes in wood are at ends of sleeve.

4. To mount quilt, line up holes in wood with nails in wall. Press dowel in place, making sure nails go into holes.

Hook-and-Loop Tape

Hook-and-loop tape (such as Velcro) provides another simple method for hanging a quilt and still allowing for it to be cleaned or laundered, because the tape is washable.

HOOK STRIP ON BACKING

1. Cut a 2″-wide strip of hook-and-loop tape 2″ shorter than quilt width.

2. Cut a 2″-wide wooden lattice strip same length as tape. Seal wood and let dry in same manner as for sleeves, above.

3. Separate the tape halves so that you have one strip with hooks (stiffer strip) and one with loops (softer strip).

4. Center the hook strip across quilt backing ½″ below top edge. Hand-sew all strip edges securely in place, making sure stitches don't show through on front of quilt.

LOOP STRIP ON LATTICE

5. Attach the loop strip to lattice, aligning edges, using a staple gun or hot glue gun.

6. Measure, mark, and affix lattice securely to wall with nails, with loop strip facing out. Place nails ½″ from lattice ends and in the center. Add nails between those already placed, dividing and subdividing spaces, using as many nails as needed to support weight of quilt.

7. To mount quilt, align hook and loop halves of tape. Press tape halves together firmly.

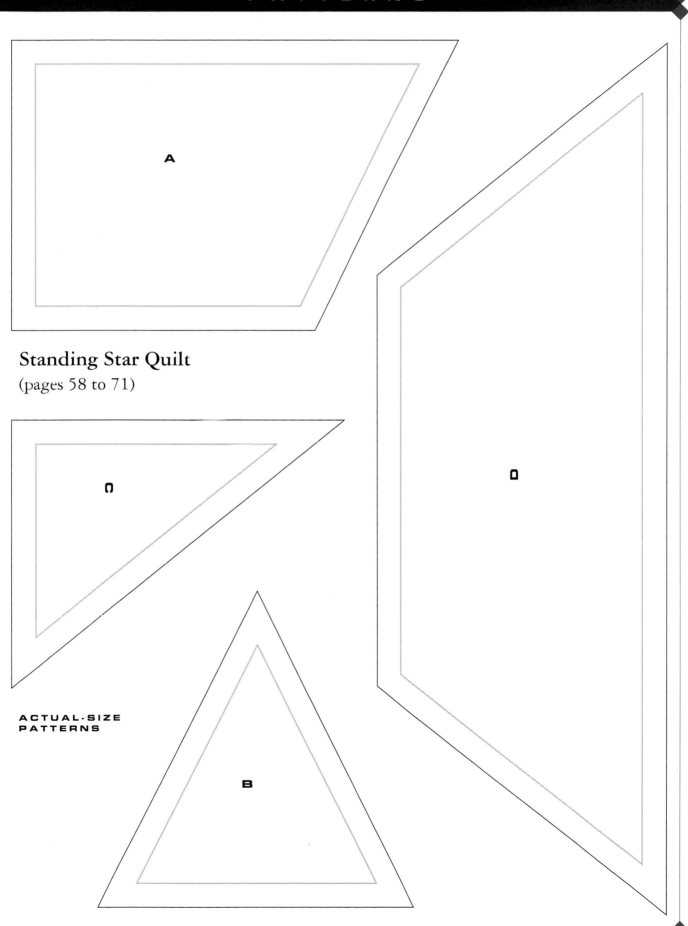

Standing Star Quilt

(pages 58 to 71)

ACTUAL-SIZE PATTERNS

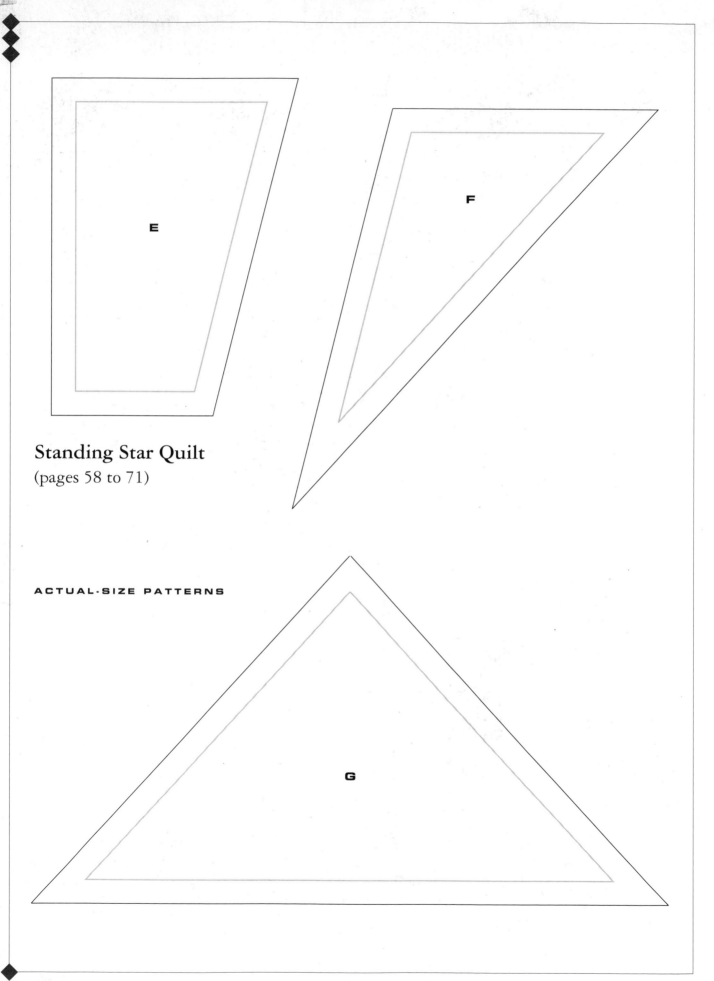

E

F

Standing Star Quilt
(pages 58 to 71)

ACTUAL·SIZE PATTERNS

G